A lady named
Faye in my church
gave this to you
after I told her
you were in the
FDNY. She hopes
you read it and
know you are
thought of with
love.

    Love,
     MOM
     2023-August 10

No Greater Love

By

Richard Damante

authorHOUSE®

AuthorHouse™
1663 Liberty Drive
Bloomington, IN 47403
www.authorhouse.com
Phone: 1 (800) 839-8640

This is a work of fiction. All of the characters, names, incidents, organizations, and dialogue in this novel are either the products of the author's imagination or are used fictitiously.

Published by AuthorHouse 08/04/2017

ISBN: 978-1-4208-0710-3 (sc)
ISBN: 978-1-4685-0971-7 (e)

Print information available on the last page.

This book is printed on acid-free paper.

All scripture quotations are from the Holy Bible, New International Version. NIV. Copyright 1973, 1978, 1984 by Intl. Bible Society

Dedicated to the Memory of All Who Perished On That Tragic September Morning.....You Are Forever In Our Hearts And Prayers. To All Who Responded To Help, And To The Ones Left Behind, God Bless You All, And May Your Hearts Be Mended.

Give me your tired, your poor, your huddled masses yearning to breathe free....Inscription on the
Statue of Liberty

"Come unto me all of you who are weary and I will give you rest"
Matthew 11:28

"All who call on the name of the Lord will be saved"
Romans 10:13

No Greater Love is a fictional work inspired by the events of September 11th, 2001. The characters in the story do not represent any particular person. All similarities are purely coincidental. The Fire Companies are also fictional. They are here to help tell a story.

TABLE OF CONTENTS

PROLOGUE

I was born and raised in New York. I was a firefighter for 10 years in two Long Island fire departments. Over that course of time I met many FDNY firefighters. Some of these men taught firefighting courses at the Nassau County Fire Services Academy in Bethpage. There was a good reason for this. These men were professionals. They taught from experience.

On September 11, 2001, I watched in horror as the events unfolded on worldwide television. I was waiting to catch a plane at Sky Harbor Airport in Phoenix. I was standing in line to buy a newspaper when I first noticed the picture on the television. A man in line told me the Trade Center was on fire. He heard that a plane had crashed into it. My response to him took him by surprise. I told him that planes don't fly over Manhattan.

My first thought was for the brave men and women who responded to this tragedy. I knew how they thought. If there were any sign of hope of helping someone, they would do it. They would put their lives on the line because that was their job. After watching the second tower get hit, I knew that this was no random accident. Five minutes later, all the television sets in the airport went blank. A hush came over the crowd. All of a sudden no one worried about whether or not his or her plane would leave on time. No, the events that were unfolding were much bigger than our own personal lives.

In the twenty minutes it took me to get home from the airport that day, the first tower had collapsed. I had just walked in the door and turned on the television just in time to see the North Tower collapse. I was devastated. I watched my city, my hometown attacked. How could anyone do such a horrible thing? How can someone hate so much?

It took me 2 months to finally get back to New York. I knew deep within myself, I must do something. I hadn't been in the Fire Service since 1990, but I wanted to be there. I wanted to help in any way that I could. God had put the whole tragic event on my heart. He also put His love, and my love for the Fire Service in there also.

On November 12, 2001, I visited Ground Zero. I took the Long Island Railroad into the city that morning not knowing what to expect. How would I react once I got there? Would it be too overwhelming? Did I make a mistake by going there? All my questions would be answered in a short while. I knew I was going to Ground Zero for a reason, but what that reason was, I did not know yet.

When I got out of the subway station I was lost. I looked up into the sky, but the towers were not there to guide me. Without them, I could not find my bearings. I finally found my way there. What I saw was horrible. Most of the scene was now fenced off. Policemen and State Troopers had formed a perimeter and no one was allowed to enter except the workers.

In all this devastation though, I felt hope for the first time. The closer I got, the sounds, sights, and smells of ground zero were prevalent. My brother in law and I started talking to a State Trooper. I told him that I had come from Arizona to pay my respects. It was then that God intervened. In a matter of minutes, this State Trooper took my brother in law and I behind the lines, and walked us into Ground Zero.

Chaos surrounded us. The closer we got to the pile; I was overcome with an emotion that I had never felt before. I felt the presence of God and His angels watching over all who came to work or visit. I knew God was there that terrible day. He was there along with His angels calling people home. Yes, the victims died a horrible death, but they were not alone. Jesus was there leading the way, holding each of them by their hands. At that moment I knew that I was on Holy Ground.

On the plane ride home, I now knew what I had to do. I knew why I had traveled over 2,500 miles. It was my duty to tell people all over the world about my brother firefighters, and about God. My first work was a play titled Rescue 3:16. This play was performed for five nights on September 5, 6, 7, 9 and 11, 2002. It was very emotional for the cast and crew to relive this event over and over during the many hours of rehearsals. It was all worthwhile though, seeing the reaction it had on all who saw the play. Many people gave their lives to the Lord, or rededicated themselves to their faith.

I wrote No Greater Love for two reasons. Many people across the nation saw what happened, but did not have a personal connection to it. This story is here to show that these people who were lost were just like you and me. They were not just a picture or a name, but a father, a brother, or a husband.

The second reason is to tell you that there is hope. My faith is what got me through it. Through bad, good will always prevail. God will get you through the rough parts in your life. He did not abandon us, or all those who were lost. He is here, and always will be.

I hope you enjoy the story. It is written out of love for my brother firefighters, and a never-ending love for our Lord and Savior Jesus Christ. Here now, the story of No Greater Love.

INTRODUCTION

SEPTEMBER 11, 2000

The sun came up just like any other day this morning. From the second story window of the firehouse, the Manhattan skyline rose out of the distance. In all their glory, stood the gleaming, proud twin towers of the World Trade Center. Even though Richie awoke every morning he was on duty to this fabulous picture before him, he never tired of the splendor of the buildings against the rising sun.

Richie's bed was the one closest to the window. He slept in the same bed every night he was on duty for the last 15 years. Being a firefighter in the FDNY was a dream come true. In spite of the pleas from his family and his wife, he was driven to realize his dream. After graduating from college, and being stuck in a few boring dead end jobs in the business world, he knew where his first love lied.

His first exposure to the fire service came one summer day back in 1973, when his dad's car caught fire in the driveway. The excitement caused by the approaching sirens and flashing red lights brought an uproar to the quiet suburban Long Island neighborhood. As flames danced out from under the hood and through the front grill of the auto, thick black smoke climbed higher and higher into the light blue sky above. Richie ran for the garden hose, and doused the last remnants of the fire right as the Chief and first due units pulled up to the scene.

The responding firefighters quickly popped open the hood and the trunk to check for any remaining fire. They disconnected the battery, and washed down the engine compartment one more time with the booster line mounted on top of the pumper. When the Chief was satisfied the fire was out, he gave the orders to return to their stations. The last truck to leave was the shiny new 100-foot aerial ladder. Richie's eyes lit up as he walked around the truck. There were axes and tools mounted on the truck, along with breathing masks, and a compliment of ladders of all different sizes.

Richie watched as the departing firefighters jumped on the back step of the ladder truck for the trip back to their station. As the truck slowly pulled away, he imagined himself someday riding on the back step to a call, and feeling the wind against his face. Yes, no matter what, someday he had to find out what it would be like. This day would change his life in many ways, but not like he or his family could ever imagine.

As usual, Richie was the first one up each morning he was on duty. The night before had been fairly uneventful. A few rubbish fires and an auto accident on the Brooklyn Queens Expressway were the only calls of the night the men of Ladder Company 179 and Engine Company 200 would respond to. They were housed together in one of the oldest buildings in Brooklyn Heights. Their quarters were small compared to some of the newer stations the city had built during the last 40 years, but none of these newer stations had the look or feel of a real New York City firehouse.

There was something to say about the Palace, as each and every member of Ladder 179 and Engine 200 called their station. These men didn't come to work like most people do. No, they didn't think of their jobs as work, but as time spent with the brothers.

They were all as close as you could get to being a family. These men all experienced life and death together. They saw more joy, but they also saw sorrow. They witnessed the miracle of life while delivering a newborn baby, and the throes of death at senseless tragedies. The unwritten law in this firehouse was the same at every firehouse across the city. What we see, say, and do here and on our calls, stays here. These men all had families. It was no use burdening them with more worries about their dangerous occupation. The men and women of the FDNY saw more fire, and more death in one week, than most departments see in ten years. The FDNY is the big leagues of firefighting. To be a member of the FDNY means you are the best of the best. All their hours of training and responding to emergencies could not prepare any of them for the events that would take place one year from today, on September 11, 2001. Their passion for the job, for helping others, and for their great city, was all that mattered. They didn't think about dying, but the threat was always there.

If they had to die though, what better way to go than doing what they loved to do? Yes, they would leave behind widows and children, but it was part of the job. No one wanted to die, but it was a part of living. Yes sir, poor Billy Smith, being taken out by a drunk driver, now that was a waste of a life. Billy was larger than life itself.

He was active in many department activities. He played bass drum in the Emerald Society Bagpipe Band, and was the starting middle linebacker on the FDNY Bravest football team. Last month, while returning home from his 6pm to 9am tour at the Palace, he was blindsided by a drunk driver only two blocks from his home. His wife was talking on the phone at the time and heard the impact. Her first thought was too bad Billy wasn't home to run out and help any way he could. Billy was killed instantly, leaving Behind his wife and three little boys. There wasn't even a scratch on the other driver.

Billy's funeral was huge. All the members of Ladder 179 and Engine 200 were there, as were many other brothers of the FDNY family. When the casket was carried out of the church the bagpipers began playing Amazing Grace. They formed a circle, leaving a space where Billy would usually stand with his bass drum. Many wept openly as they played. As his flag draped casket was lifted atop the Engine of the volunteer fire department he also belonged to, all the firefighters present saluted. They were all dressed in their crisp navy blue Class A uniforms. His youngest son wore his dad's helmet proudly. Daddy wouldn't be coming home anymore, but his "uncles" from both fire departments would make sure the boys would never be without a dad.

CHAPTER 1

It was now 8am and the firehouse was full of life with men coming on and off duty. The building was an old narrow three- story brownstone built in the early 1900's. Many of the buildings around the firehouse had been renovated in recent years and sold for millions of dollars to stock brokers, lawyers, and bankers who enjoyed the short subway ride to work in lower Manhattan. Yes, the neighborhood had changed over the years. Many years ago immigrants from Italy, Ireland, and Scandinavia came to America and called this neighborhood home. Very rarely now did you hear the native tongues of the early immigrants spoken. It was replaced by the banter of these young wealthy professionals speaking about their investment portfolios. Many of the firefighters assigned to the Palace were the grandsons and great-grandsons of the early immigrants who built, lived, and worked in the neighborhood.

Richard Damante

They had names like Demarco, Donovan, Daly, and Giordano. Their families had moved from the area for the greener pastures of Long Island. There was something about the neighborhood though that would always make it feel special. Everyone who ever lived there felt pride because it was built on the sweat, blood and dreams of their ancestors.

They came to America with pennies in their pockets. The Land of Opportunity lay ahead of them. They were mostly laborers who knew that hard work was not a sin. They were masons, ironworkers, workers, and fishermen. They were dockworkers and welders who built ships and worked a few blocks away at the old Brooklyn Navy Yard. They were proud to be Americans now, and many of them sent sons off to war to defend their new country. In one word, they were proud - proud of their heritage, their accomplishments, and their new families in America. There was no looking back. America was now their new home, and Brooklyn was their identity.

As Richie walked down the stairs from the second floor bunkroom to the firehouse dayroom he passed by history. The history was told by the dozens of photographs that lined the walls on both sides of the stairwell. Ladder 179 and Engine 200 were two of the first companies organized that made up the old Brooklyn Fire

Department. The photos were of every member, and every piece of fire apparatus that ever served at the station. Each picture told a story. There were the company Christmas parties, the company picnics, and wedding celebrations. There were the pictures of many of the calls the companies had responded to over the years. Proudly displayed were all the unit citations both companies had received over the years.

As he spotted his own picture on the wall, Richie once again felt that feeling of pride and of being part of something good, his firehouse family. Oh how he loved his job. The pay could have been a lot better, but what the heck. Many people his own age sold out to the almighty dollar and hated their jobs, but not Richie DeMarco. No, he was his own man. He was a man of integrity, outstanding family values, and a man of faith.

"Good Morning L.T., did you sleep good last night?"

"I slept like a baby Richie. I can't remember the last night tour I worked where we didn't have a call past midnight."

"It's probably because today is the first day of school, summer break is over...no more fooling around at night," Richie replied.

Richard Damante

As Richie started to prepare breakfast for the guys, the house began to come alive. During the next hour both crews and their officers would be heading home and the fresh crews would start the day all over again. In all the firehouses across the five boroughs of the city this same scenario would be playing out. Even though the new shift didn't officially begin until 9am, many of the guys would get to their stations early to shoot the breeze and to find out what calls the companies responded to the night before. All firefighters were alike. They never wanted to miss a call.

At any given time, ten firefighters and two officers manned the Palace. Every morning this number doubled as the shift change occurred. It was not uncommon for 24 men to be cramped into the small kitchen talking about the results of the previous nights Yankee or Met game. Only a city this large had two of every professional sports team.

The firefighters on duty today would clean the firehouse in the morning. They all had assigned jobs. The senior men had the more desirable jobs while the rookies, or probies as they were called, usually were relegated to latrine duty. A probie is a probationary firefighter with less than one full year of service. Once the day chores were completed there were usually building and fire hydrant inspections, drill time, and of course shopping time to buy the food that was needed to prepare the days meals. Most stations had assigned cooks, but every now and then, depending who was on duty, they might have take-out instead of a fresh cooked meal. The cost of the meal would be divided up between how many guys were going to be eating. The city provided the room and board. When it came to meals, and the pots and pans needed to cook them, the firefighters were on their own dime.

Richie came from a large Italian family. Two things usually occur when you are born into a large Italian family. Number one, you like to eat, as eating usually turns into a social event. It is not uncommon for an Italian mother to prepare a meal for twelve people even though she knows her immediate family consists of only five people. Secondly, and invariably, Italians all know how to cook, and take pride in it. Richie was no exception. His mother taught him cooking was a labor of love. He held onto this idea when he was probationary firefighter, and for the last fifteen years did all of the cooking at the station when he was on duty.

CHAPTER 2

OCTOBER 11, 2000

New Yorkers everywhere were caught in a feverish pitch. For the first time in almost 50 years a Subway Series was on the horizon. Yes, the beloved New York Yankees, and the underdog New York Mets might actually play each other in the World Series. Growing up, Richie always dreamed what it would be like having an all New York World Series. Back in the early 1970's both teams had one thing in common, neither of them were any good. The Mets would show flashes of greatness. They even made it to the series in 1973 and lost to Oakland, but they couldn't string together winning seasons. The Yankees were the team of tradition. Of Ruth, Gehrig, DiMaggio, and Mantle, but those days were behind them. For ten years from 1965 to 1975 the Yankees were a different club. When Richie was 8 years old his dad took him to the old Yankee Stadium to see his first ballgame. What a place. There is no other stadium like Yankee Stadium. The stadium lies in the Bronx, amidst tenements, abandoned buildings, and the Bronx House of Detention.

Grass growing in the Bronx is among itself a miracle. Seeing the neatly manicured bright green grass of Yankee Stadium was locked in this 8 year old's mind forever. The stadium was truly breathtaking. The unique stadium façade that gave Yankee Stadium its identity was awesome. It was one thing to see it in pictures, on baseball cards, and on T.V. Seeing it and experiencing it in person, was something to brag about to all his friends in the neighborhood.

Richie got to see Mickey Mantle play that day. The Mick, as most New Yorkers called him, was nearing the end of his playing career. He was relegated to playing first base. In his prime Mickey Mantle could run down any ball hit into the huge centerfield of Yankee Stadium. Now, with both knees shot, chasing ground balls was a chore for Mantle. What a pity. A career cut short by injuries and self-abuse.

It was 10pm and the crews of Ladder 179 and Engine 200 had just returned to quarters from a 10-26. A 10-26 in FDNY radio vernacular is short for food burning on the stove. The crews felt lucky that the call turned out to be nothing. They started their night tour at 6pm and it was an unusually busy night. On duty with Richie tonight were Lieutenant Jack Farley, and firefighters Joey Donovan, Vinny Amarosa, Louie Ludwig, and Bobby Giordano. These six men made up the crew of Ladder 179. On duty in Engine 200 were Captain Bill Shields and firefighters Willy Johnson, Jimmy Daly, Bobbie York, Jim Lennon, and Ralphie Chiarello. Ralphie had joined the department only two months earlier. He seemed like an ok kid, even though he was a bit cocky. The guys would cure him of that though. These men knew what buttons to push, and just how far to push them.

"Hey Richie, are we gonna eat anytime soon tonight or what?" Ralphie shouted as the men began to get out of their bunker gear.

"I'm starving, I haven't had anything to eat since I got up this morning. Its been like, 12 hours I think," he continued.

"Twelve hours kid....that would mean you got up this morning at about 10 o'clock you lazy bum," Richie chimed in.

Bobby York heard the conversation as he passed by and began to laugh. "Hey, leave the kid alone Richie. He's our probie not yours. He belongs to the Engine Company. If anyone gets to break his chops, its us." They all had a good laugh and headed to the kitchen.

The kitchen was a long narrow room located at the rear of the station behind the apparatus floor. A big cast iron stove and an old stainless steel refrigerator were off to the right. To the left were two long wooden tables with mismatched checkerboard tablecloths. This is where the men ate their meals. The kitchen table was also a place to joke about everything and anything. You had to have a thick skin at times, but it was all done in good fun. Everyone was fair game, even your family members. You could poke fun at how someone looked, or how they talked. You could talk about a guy's wife, or girlfriend, but don't ever cross the line and talk about a guy's mother. She was off limits to everyone.

If you were picked on it meant you were accepted. The Palace had its fair share of prima donnas over the years who could dish it out, but not take it. This crew though was the exception. No one had big egos here. You had to leave it at the front door if you had one.

In a matter of minutes, the aroma of grilled onions began to fill the kitchen. Richie had planned to cook a meatloaf and mashed potatoes tonight. Those plans quickly changed when the first alarm bells sounded at 6:10pm. No, there would be no meatloaf tonight. Hamburgers and French fries would now be tonight's dinner menu. No one would complain; they were all too hungry to wait for a meatloaf to cook.

When the last of the dishes were cleaned off the table, the alarm bells began to ring again. Vinny Amarosa shouted the address over the P.A. system. Vinny was on house-watch, and it was his job to log in all the calls that the companies responded to. Each firefighter would take turns doing this throughout the day.

As the crews scrambled into their gear the roar of the diesel engines came to life. Each rig had its own unique engine sound. Engine 200 had a high pitch while Ladder 179 had a deep bass roar. Captain Shields hit the buttons on the wall to open the big red bay doors. Lieutenant Jack Farley jumped into the cab of Ladder 179 and began to read the printout of the address. One Twenty Two Middagh Street. It was a short ride from the Palace. Just by reading the address Lieutenant Farley knew that it was an occupied multiple dwelling. He had worked in Brooklyn Heights his whole career and knew every building in the area.

Engine 200 would lead the way, with Ladder 179 following close behind. These two companies would be the first due units at the address. It was standard operating procedure for the Engine to drop a line at the closest fire hydrant, and pull off to the front of the building.

As the rigs pulled out of the Palace, they made a quick right onto Henry Street, and made their way down the narrow passage. These streets were old, and built before the dawn of SUVs. Parked cars lined both sides of the street, making the driver's job extremely difficult at times. In the back of every chauffeur's mind, they always feared some little kid running out from in-between the parked cars and not having enough time to jam on the brakes.

Willie Johnson was behind the wheel of 200 tonight. He was a 23- year veteran and an excellent pump operator. Joey Donovan was Driving 179. The men always kidded him about how slow he drove to calls. It was not uncommon for the Engine to be a full two blocks ahead of the Ladder Truck by the time they got to the scene.

As Engine 200 got closer to the scene, Captain Shields notified the responding units that heavy black smoke was visible. He knew that they had a "job". A job is what the men called a working fire. Ladder 179 heard the transmission and could now see the smoke for themselves. Each man began to mask up and get ready for some more action. The neighborhood was now alive with the flashing lights and blazing sirens of the approaching units. To some people in the neighborhood, a fire was free entertainment.

Engine 200 made a left onto Middagh Street and came to a rolling stop. Ralphie Chiarello jumped out of the crew compartment and ran around the rig to the rear step. He jumped up and grabbed the big four-inch feeder line and began to pull it off. He was the hydrant man tonight. It was his job to make sure that the hose would be hooked up to the hydrant and supply the 500 gallons of water per minute that Engine 200 was capable of pumping. As soon as he wrapped the hose around the base of the hydrant and placed his boot on top of it, he gave a "thumbs up" sign and Engine 200 sped down the block to the front of the building. Ralphie quickly unscrewed the cap off of the cast iron hydrant. He stuck his spanner wrench into the opening to make sure it was clear of debris. It was not uncommon for some kids to shove beer cans in there as a joke. It might have seemed like harmless fun to them, but it could cost a firefighter his life if the water didn't come when it was needed.

As he threaded the hose onto the hydrant, Ralphie's adrenaline began to flow. Once given the signal from Joey Donovan to charge the line, he would wind the spanner wrench as fast as he could to open the valve and let the water flow. The flat four-inch hose would now slowly come to life like a slithering snake. As the water filled the hose, it found its way to the waiting pumper. His job was done. He would now mask up and be prepared to be the backup man on a second hose line if needed.

The street was filled with the shouts of neighbors pointing to the third floor apartment. The fire had already vented itself through the front bay window. The bright orange and yellow flames danced skyward against the blackness of the night.

Richie and the crew entered the smoke filled building. The tenants were fleeing, carrying what they considered to be their valuables; things that they could not afford to lose in the fire. Television sets, VCR's, and stereos seemed to be what these people cared about the most.

Richie and Louie Ludwig were the forcible entry and search team tonight. These two men had been in many of the same situations like this one before. They had a sixth sense as to the others whereabouts in a fire. As they approached the stairwell, a man and woman grabbed Louie and pleaded with them that their baby was still upstairs, trapped behind a wall of thick black smoke in their third floor apartment. How odd, Richie thought, that they were both carrying possessions from their apartment, but left their child behind. Louie and Richie raced up the stairs two at a time. They each carried their forcible entry tools. Richie carried an axe and a halligan tool, while Louie had a six-foot hook. By the time they reached the 2nd floor landing, they had to stop to don the facemasks of their air tanks.

The building was typical of most of the neighborhood brownstones, or railroad flats as they were sometimes called. There was the sub basement, or ground floor, which was just below street level, and three stories above. It was attached to other brownstones on each side, with windows facing the front and back of the building. All the tenants shared a common entry, and the stairs ran up the inside of the building with a landing on each floor. Any firewalls or firebreaks built into these buildings many years earlier were long gone, due to the many renovations that had taken place over the years.

While Richie and Louie proceeded up past the advancing hose line, Bobby Giordano climbed up the rear fire escape. It was his job to vent the fire, but only when the Engine Company was ready to get water on it. If he took out the windows too soon, the influx of oxygen would cause the fire to grow and flashover. Even though fire scenes resembled utter chaos, the actions of the firefighters were very precise. Each depended on the other not only to do their jobs, but also to do it at the right time.

The Engine Company had now advanced to the third floor landing. Each man was now on his hands and knees due to the heavy smoke and heat condition. Fires are hot enough as it is. Add forty pounds of heavy turnout gear and tools, and it is amazing how anyone can do this job for a living. "Charge the line," Captain Shields shouted over his radio to Willie Johnson, who was outside manning the pump. In a matter of seconds, the line was charged and ready to advance into the burning apartment. Bobby York cracked open the nozzle and water sprayed out before him. Captain Shields shouted the order to advance, and he, Bobby, and Jimmy Daly duck walked the hose to the apartment door.

Only seconds before, Richie and Louie had entered the apartment. They knew there was some child still in there. They radioed this information to Bobby Giordano who took out the rear windows with his ax. He immediately got a face full of thick black poisonous smoke and began to cough. He then crawled inside the broken window into the dark hole. There was absolutely no visibility. The light on his helmet, and the one attached to his turnout coat was useless in a fire like this.

He had to go on instinct and his sense of touch and feel. It was the same for Richie and Louie at the opposite end of the apartment. They both crawled into the apartment and began their search.

With one hand on the wall, they followed each other into the first room. They dragged their legs and their tools, kicking and feeling for furniture or a victim. They hugged the wall with their right hand so they would net get lost or disoriented. Their experience taught them little kids are usually found in one of three places, under the bed, in the bathtub, or in their own beds. At other fires they had received reports of babies or children trapped in fires, and the baby turned out to be twenty-five years old. Yes they were someone's baby, but not a baby.

After a thorough search of the first room, they proceeded to the next one. When they got to the archway between the two rooms, they saw the warm red glow of the fire across the ceiling. The room and all of its contents were completely in flames. They quickly passed the fire and entered the third room. It was there that they found her. Little Rebecca was only three years old. Louie found her still under the covers clutching her stuffed bear. He quickly tore off the sheets and carried her to the rear of the apartment. He knew by now that Bobby Giordano should be there.

Richard Damante

Bobby heard the muffled shouts of Richie and Louie through his mask. He had just finished searching the rear room of the apartment. In the blackness, all three of the firefighters bumped into each other. They crawled to the open window and out of the apartment. Louie carried little Rebecca out onto the fire escape and immediately started CPR on her lifeless body. She looked peaceful, just like she was sleeping.

The Engine Company was now busy dousing the flames. They wouldn't stop soaking the room until the last burning ember was extinguished. Once they were satisfied the fire was out, they would pick up the hose lines and pat themselves on the back for another job well done. In all the excitement, they didn't even know about Rebecca until they got down to the street.

She was placed in the back of the ambulance and taken to Long Island College Hospital. A few minutes later she was pronounced dead by the Emergency Room attending physician. What a tragedy and a senseless loss of life. Why? Why did bad things happen in the world? Why did bad things happen to little children? Why did people run out of burning buildings with television sets and leave their kids behind?

Richie asked himself these same questions at every tragedy he came across in the last fifteen years. Seeing little children die was unnatural. Old people die, but not little children. Why? Only God knew the answer. Richie would have to rely on his faith to get him through this. Oh how his life had changed in the last three years. Three years ago he devoted his life to God and found a new strength and power. Sure there were still good days and bad days, but he and his family knew they didn't have to live life alone. With Jesus, all things were possible.

CHAPTER 3

November 11, 2000

The subway series was now over and the Yankees were celebrating yet another world championship. The Mets had put up a good fight, but fell short once again. Little did anyone know how the subway series helped lay the groundwork for a united New York City. New Yorkers once again felt pride in their great city. Ten months from now, their mettle, and their faiths, would be tested like no other time in history.

The Mets were New York's blue-collar team, while the Yankees were the Park Avenue millionaires. If you were a true New Yorker you rooted for one team or the other. Even though both teams played in different leagues, your allegiance was to one team and one team only. It was the same with the Jets and Giants, Rangers and Islanders, and Knicks and the Nets. Forget the teams from Buffalo. Those teams may have well been in a different state altogether.

When the Dodgers and Giants moved to the west coast in the late 1950's, the city was left with only one major league baseball team, the Yankees. The Yankees broke the hearts of many Dodger and Giant fans over the years. Many of these fans could never get themselves to root for the Yankees. How could they like a team they learned to hate? In 1962, an expansion team was granted to New York. They would be in the National League and be called the New York Metropolitan Baseball Club, or Mets for short. Many of the old Dodger and Giant fans now pledged their allegiance to the new team.

In just seven short years their beloved Mets, or amazing Mets, as many dubbed them, would do the impossible and become World Champions. Each year, the onset of spring would bring the start of a new baseball season, and the dream of another subway series. These dreams usually were snuffed out by mid May due to the fortunes or misfortunes of one team or the other. It would take 38 years for the subway series to return to the big apple, but it was worth the wait.

Jane DeMarco was a Mets fan at heart. Her dad was one of those old Dodger fans who could never get himself to root for the Yankees. He instilled this belief in his daughter. She was a petite attractive blonde with sparkling blue eyes. She had met Richie over 20 years ago. After only a few months of dating, they knew they wanted to spend the rest of their lives together. She loved being a part of Richie's big extended family. They welcomed her into their ever-growing family.

It was not uncommon for the relatives to just drop by and say hello. Before you knew it, phone calls were made and a small intimate get together would turn into a feast for a king. Like all good Italian families, the DeMarcos enjoyed breaking bread together, and being a part of each other's lives. They truly loved one another, and it showed. The hardest thing for Jane was trying to remember everyone's names, and who belonged to which Aunt or Uncle. When she finally knew who was who, the family got even larger with the weddings and births of cousins, grandchildren, and great grandchildren.

It was through his family that Richie learned his values. His dad always taught him family is family through good and bad. Never turn your back on anyone who needed your help, that's what a family was for. It was there for love and support. Growing up he always knew his parents would be there for him, and it was now his turn to pass on these values to his own children.

After five years of marriage, Jane and Richie were blessed with the birth of twins. Instantly the size of their family doubled. Thomas was born first, and two minutes later his twin sister Amanda followed. It was truly love at first sight when Richie held the babies in his arms for the very first time. Most people leave the hospital with one baby, why was he so blessed to be leaving with two.

Fourteen years later he felt the same way as he did the day they were born. Sure, there were difficult times, but it all was worth it. He could never imagine what life would be like without Jane and the twins. They were a happy family with a special bond that held them together. It was a special bond of love, and of their faith in God.

This chilly autumn day was no exception. After doing family chores all morning the kids would be going to church to take part in one of their many youth group activities. Weekends were always a busy time around the house, but they always found time for God and for each other. Today would be no exception.

After a busy day the family would drive to Aunt Carol's house for a party. It was cousin Vicki's 19th birthday. "Hey dad, how many more years are you gonna be a firefighter," Tommy asked his father. "That depends on a lot of things son, I don't know, at least five so I can put in my twenty years, but maybe ten more years. I'm still young....besides; the bills don't go away just because you retire. "Dad, you know I worry about you every time you go to work. Think about us too, okay." Amanda was very close to her dad and he knew what she just said came from her heart. "Sometimes I wish you had a regular job like most dads, but I also know that I'm proud of what you do."

"Thanks Amanda, you know I love my job kids, and I also love you and your mom." Richie reached over and held Jane's hand as he drove down the busy street. Jane smiled and gave Richie a little wink. She looked over her shoulder at the twins and began to speak. "I know how you feel kids. I worry about your dad all the time, but I know his job makes him happy, besides; look at all the extra time he gets to spend with us. If he had a regular job in the city we would hardly see him during the week. I have confidence in him. He's a great firefighter and he knows what he is doing, and don't forget what he always tells us. He has a special angel watching over him." They all laughed and continued their conversation. It helped pass the time as they made their way through the weekend shopping traffic. In a few weeks, the onset of the Christmas season would make traffic even worse.

Everyone had a good time at the party. After dinner it was time to relax. "Hey Grandma, did you hear my dad's gonna retire in five years," Tommy shouted out. All eyes in the room now focused on Richie. "That's not quite what I said Tommy. We were discussing this on the way over here tonight. What I said was in five years I'll have my 20 years on the job, but I'm not looking to retire any time soon." "Oh, I wish you would now. You know how your dad and I feel about it. We never wanted you to do it in the first place. You should retire and get yourself a normal job."

Richie got up and walked over to his mom and put his hand on her shoulder. "That's just it mom, I don't want a normal job. I feel like what I do is worthwhile. Like I make a difference. I just can't get that same feeling in the business world. I feel like God gave me a gift, a second chance. Sure this job is hard at times, but it's a big part of me. I just can't give it up. Not right now."

It was now almost an hour past midnight. The party had broken up at 10:00pm and everyone had returned home. It was a very busy day and everyone went right to bed. After sleeping for a while it happened. Jane awoke suddenly knowing something was wrong. Richie was grimacing and talking in his sleep, but she could not make out what he was saying. This was not the first time this had happened. It was the reoccurring dream once again. Jane reached over and woke her husband up.

"Richie...Richie...are you okay," she said nervously. He did not respond right away. After a few more times of asking him the same question, Richie awoke. "What....ah..ah..Jane...oh, thank God."

"Richie, what is it, the dream again?"

"Yeah, I can't get the picture of her out of my mind. She was so young. So little. If only we had gotten to her sooner."

"Its not your fault Richie. You did everything you could that night. Why are you blaming yourself?"

"We were tired Jane. It was a busy night, but we should have split up. We knew she was in the apartment."

This was not the first time in his career that Richie experienced the death of a child. For some reason though, he took this one the hardest. It had been one month since they found Rebecca's lifeless body. Her death was hard to accept.

Rebecca would make the headlines in every New York City newspaper. She was a foster child who had recently been placed in a new home. Her foster parents were now coming under media attack. Even the firefighters were being scrutinized.

As Richie lay there weeping, Jane clenched his hand and began to pray out loud. "Dear Father, I ask you for peace. Please bring your peace to Richie tonight. I ask you Father God to remove the guilt that Richie and the other firefighters are feeling over the death of little Rebecca. We know Rebecca is wrapped up in your loving arms right now, and know there is no better place for her to be, Lord. Continue to love us, watch over us, and guide us. In Jesus name we pray, Amen."

It was a short prayer but a meaningful one. One meant to bring peace. Just hearing the words made Richie feel better. He knew that having Jesus Christ as his Savior helped comfort him and his family through times like this. Yes, deep down inside he knew that he and his buddies did everything they could that night to save Rebecca. He also knew that terrible things happen to good people, but it was not his job to ask God why. Only God Himself knew the answer.

Many times, when Richie would talk to other firefighters about God, he would get the same answers. It's not that they didn't believe in God, but they questioned their own faith. Many of them kept God at a distance. He was there if they needed Him, but many chose to walk through life alone. Every time they experienced something bad they would think about God in both a negative and positive way. Rebecca's death would be a new beginning in their lives. They all had seen death on the job before, but never had they taken it so personally. God was beginning to prepare each of them for something much bigger. Yes, Rebecca would not die in vain. Her death was part of God's big plan. Every life has a meaning, and only God knows what that meaning is.

CHAPTER 4

December 11, 2000

The New York Daily News was a staple of every firehouse in the city. It was an old newspaper, and synonymous with New York City. An article in today's paper caught the attention of every member of Engine 200 and Ladder 179. Due to public outcry, the mayor's office had launched a probe into Rebecca's death.

According to the article, the investigation would be thorough and wide reaching. The whole Child Protective Services Division would be examined under a microscope. As it turns out, Rebecca's foster parents had already been part of a previous investigation two years earlier. The investigation would not bring Rebecca back, but hopefully, it might prevent the death of any other children.

In addition to Child Protective Services, the New York City Police Department, the Emergency Services Division, and the Fire Department would also be investigated. Both the Fire and Police Department unions labeled the investigation a witch-hunt. They knew that they followed department procedure and did nothing wrong the night of Rebecca's death. It looked to them that someone was trying to cover up their own mistakes and were trying to blame the death on someone else.

Captain Shields was in his office when the phone rang. "Fire Department, Captain Shields. Yes... ok...ok...no, I'm sorry I can't. Yeah, if you have a problem call Department Headquarters in Brooklyn," and then he slammed down the phone. Since word of the investigation spread through the various media outlets, everyone wanted to speak to the men who responded to the fire that night. Each man of Engine 200 and Ladder 179 was instructed not to talk to the media. Nothing good could come of it. The reporters and writers were all looking for a story, and the Department was not going to be dragged through the mud.

Firefighters are a private bunch. They tend to internalize their emotions. Even though they were all saddened by Rebecca's death, deep down they knew they were not to blame. Yes, even Ralphie Chiarello felt saddened that night. Did he do his best? Did he follow the right procedures? Every time the answer came back yes, but he still felt responsible. If only they had gotten water on the fire sooner, maybe, just maybe, she would still be alive.

All firefighters play a life and death game. Each man would have to deal with his own emotions in whatever way was the best for him. Losing someone in a fire was personal, especially if it happened on your watch. Losing a child was even worse.

Thirteen years earlier Richie carried the lifeless body of a child from a suspicious fire. The fire was so intense, that when the first units arrived, all they could do was attack it from the outside. The building's owner had the fire deliberately set, and all for greed. Some of the tenants were behind in their rent and he knew by law, it would take months to have them evicted. If a little fire broke out the family would be forced to move out sooner.

It was easy to find someone to set the fire. People made careers as arsonists. Arsonists don't set fires for the money though. They do it for the thrill. The more fires they set, the thrill just isn't the same anymore. As time goes by, they need to find a bigger thrill. They change the way they set the fires, and hope to get the ultimate thrill. That is what happened in this fire.

The person who set this fire was no exception. Pete Mitchell set fires to vacant buildings for insurance claims. He was paid a flat fee for his services. Getting caught was not an option, so he had to cover his tracks. Over the years, he learned which accelerants worked the best, and which ones were the hardest to detect.

Pete had been setting fires for six years and was getting bored. He wanted more excitement. Watching his handy-work in vacant buildings wasn't exciting enough anymore. Pete wanted to play the game with a new set of rules. The new game would include people's lives. He wanted to see how big of a fire he could set without getting anyone hurt, and without getting caught.

For $500.00 Pete took the job at 4961 Hoyt Street. The buildings' owner told him to make sure the job was done during the day when the tenants were either at work or at school. Pete had other plans though. Once he received the money, it was his game. He made all the rules now.

After two weeks it was time for him to do his dirty work. At around two in the morning, Pete walked into the lobby of the building. He knew from the owner that the front lock hadn't been working for months. After he entered he quickly doused the second floor landing with a mixture of gasoline and diesel fuel. The gasoline would burn quickly and spread the fire. The diesel fuel would then ignite and burn slow and hot. It would also cause a much more severe smoke condition. He then went down the basement and did the same thing.

This fire would be different than all the others. He wouldn't even try to hide his tracks on this one. This fire would be his best one yet. He wanted excitement and he was going to get it even if it cost someone his or her life. Mitchell didn't care about the firefighters or the people who lived in the building. He only cared about himself. He knew if he stuck to the owners' original plan, all it would be was just another fire. No, he would raise the ante now, and too bad if anyone got in his way. The rules had just changed.

Shortly after 2:20 am, the alarm bells began to ring at the Palace. Engine 200 and Ladder 179 raced to the scene. The glow of the fire was visible in the night sky from half a mile away. Upon arrival, a second alarm was transmitted, and then minutes later, a third alarm. The fire was so intense it quickly spread throughout the building. The people never had a chance. In all, seven people perished that night, the youngest being a five-month-old infant. It was the first fatal fire of Richie's career, and one he would never forget.

Two days later, Pete Mitchell was arrested and charged with the murders of seven people, including one firefighter. It seems, shortly after he heard what had happened, the buildings owner got a conscious and turned in Mitchell. In exchange for his testimony the Brooklyn District Attorney would not pursue the death penalty against him. Seven lives were lost all for a few months rent.

Pete Mitchell showed no remorse throughout his trial. At his sentencing hearing the relatives of the deceased were allowed to address the court. Mitchell smirked at each of them. His final words to the judge were not for forgiveness. They were of his regret that there would be no more fires for him to set. His career was over, but he was proud of final accomplishment. His remarks were the final touches of his defense teams insanity plea. There would be no death penalty for Mitchell. One day he would realize what he had done. Maybe then, he would feel the flames of his own eternity. Sooner or later, we all will face the consequences of our actions. We all will have eternal life. It is up to us where we will spend it.

The company Christmas party was being held once again at Giovanni's Cucina Siciliana. It was a small family restaurant that had been part of the neighborhood for almost 100 years. It was owned and operated by the same family all these years. The Margulo family had migrated to the United States in 1903. Giovanni Margulo and his wife Angelina came to Ellis Island with only the clothes on their backs, and what little money they had saved.

They came to America from a little fishing town in Sicily named Licata. They came here with a dream. Their dream was to open a restaurant. They settled into an apartment at 145 Hicks Street. The ground floor was vacant space that could be turned into a restaurant. Giovanni and Angelina worked around the clock in various jobs to save enough money to pay for the deposit, and renovations needed to see their dream come to life.

The restaurant was longer, than it was wide . It was a quaint little place featuring the recipes of Angelina's old world specialties. Due to the large number of Italian immigrants in the area, Giovanni's was a huge success. The décor was plain and simple. There were small wooden rectangular tables with red and white linen table clothes. Each day Angelina would place fresh flowers on every table. The floor was made of hard oak boards that Giovanni had installed himself. It was always very shiny, and clean. On the walls were pictures featuring the beauty and warmth of Sicily.

The ceiling is what gave the restaurant its unique appeal. As was the custom at the turn of the century, the ceiling was made of embossed rolled tin. It had a very intricate design and was very ornate. Giovanni painted it with the brightest white paint he could find. Three hanging light fixtures gave the place its intimate ambiance. Almost 100 years later, Giovanni's still had the same old world appeal, nothing fancy, just great food, at good prices.

Over the years the prices may have changed, but the menu stayed the same. In 1960, Giovanni and Angelina's oldest son Anthony took over the daily operation of the restaurant. His parents still lived above the restaurant, in the same apartment they had lived in since first coming to America. On the third floor lived Anthony and his wife Lucille. The Margulo family now owned the building. It was the only place Anthony had ever lived. Three generations had now called it home. Over the last thirty years, some of the family had moved to Staten Island, but most of the family hadn't strayed more than a few blocks from home.

Annemarie Margulo was the youngest grandchild of Giovanni and Angelina. She was also the only granddaughter. She was born in 1967 and was the first family member to graduate from college. The whole Margulo family was very proud of her. Her weekends were spent helping the family run the business. Monday through Friday she worked as an investment broker at 1 World Trade Center in Manhattan. Her colleagues teased her about her loyalty to her family, but she wouldn't have it any other way. She realized the sacrifices her grandparents and parents had made for her, and this was her way of saying thank you. Her dad always tried to pay her for her time, but she wouldn't think of it. Blood was thicker than water, and besides, she enjoyed the work, and being around her family.

The men stationed at the Palace were frequent visitors of Giovanni's. Over the years, the Margulo family became part of the Engine 200 and Ladder 179 family. They had catered weddings, christenings, graduations, and all types of parties for many of the men.

On the 2nd Friday of each December, the restaurant would close its doors to the public and host the Palace Christmas Party. For the last five years, Anthony Margulo didn't even charge them. It was his way of giving back to the men that protected his neighborhood. The Christmas party was a time for everyone to come together with their wives or girlfriends and share some good times away from the daily grind of their job. The night tour this evening would be covered by firefighters from other houses in the Battalion. It was the highlight of the year, and no one wanted to miss it.

Anthony and Lucille spent all week preparing the food for tonight's feast. The buffet would include trays of mouth watering Italian delicacies such as Lasagna, Sausage and Peppers, Eggplant Parmigiana, and Anthony's famous Calamari. For dessert, Lucille spent all day baking Cannolis and Tiramisu. If you went home hungry after a party like this, it was your own fault.

Richie and Jane were among the first to arrive and were greeted at the door by Annemarie. Over the years she had gotten to know all of the firefighters by their first names. "Hi Richie, glad you could make it tonight. How are you doing Jane?"

"I'm just fine Annemarie. How are you and that beautiful little son of yours?" "Oh, that beautiful little son of mine isn't so little anymore. Joey just turned ten last week. He's growing up right before my eyes."

"Enjoy him while you can," Jane responded, "They grow up so fast these days."

Annemarie was a single mother. She was only married for a short time, to her High School sweetheart. One day he left for work in the morning, and never came back. There were rumors of foul play all over the neighborhood. Two months later he came back and asked for a divorce. Annemarie knew the marriage was shaky at best, but she was still angry. The anger she felt was not for what he did to her, but how he abandoned his little child. How could he just leave his son like that? What would she tell him when he got older, that Daddy didn't love him either anymore. When the divorce was final, he relinquished all his parental rights to the boy. The only father Joey would ever know was his grandfather. His dad moved to California and never returned. He said Brooklyn and the neighborhood was holding him back. No one ever heard from him again.

Over the years, many of the single men in the neighborhood, and at the Palace had their eye on Annemarie. She had promised herself not to get involved with another man until her son was grown up. She blamed herself for the person she chose to be Joey's dad. In the back of her mind, she worried if another relationship didn't work out, how it would affect her son. Lately, she had begun to let her guard down, and everyone knew that Ralphie Chiarello and her had taken a fondness for one another. Even her father Anthony approved of it, and he did everything in his power to see the two of them together. Yes, she liked Ralphie, but it would just have to wait for now.

Even though he knew what she was thinking, this did not deter Ralphie in the least. No, this time it was different. He loved everything about her. The men at the Palace were constantly kidding him about the age difference between himself and Annemarie. She was five years older, and the men wouldn't let Ralphie forget it. Some of them kidded him out of jealousy. Ralphie knew he was falling in love with this woman, and he would not let her slip away.

After a few hours of eating, drinking, and dancing, the party had split up into little groups. There was a group of wives in one corner, their husbands in the other corner, and a few groups that were comprised of both men and their wives.

Jane sat down next to Louie Ludwig's wife Theresa, while Richie slipped away with some of the other guys. "Hi Theresa, I have to ask you a question. How is Louie doing these days?"

"I'm so glad you asked Jane, I've never seen him like this. He's not sleeping or eating much. Christmas is a few weeks away and he doesn't even care. This Rebecca thing has really gotten to him."

"I know, it has gotten to Richie too, and I don't know why. He never reacted like this in the past. He knows he's not to blame, but it's like he is searching for answers."

Theresa's lips began to tremble as tears started to well up in her eyes. "I wish there was something I could do to help Louie. I hate seeing him like this."

"Hang in there Theresa, have faith that God has a plan. I know it's hard to do when you see your husband suffering, but remember, God is always in control."

Across the room, Richie, Louie, and Bobby Giordano were having their own conversation. They also were talking about Rebecca.

"You know, I can't get her out of my mind. I lie there awake, just seeing her face."

"Yeah, me too Bobby," Louie replied. "I think I'm going crazy. I didn't even know the kid. I've been on this job for 21 years and have never felt like this before. I don't know why either. It's frustrating."

"I've been praying about this a lot lately," Richie chimed in. "Trying to find out why she's been on our minds. I feel like God is trying to tell us something, preparing us for something maybe, but I don't know what."

"Well, I gotta tell you something Richie, I've been praying a lot too. I don't go to church every Sunday though, so I hope God is hearing my prayers too."

"Bobby, He hears your prayers and everyone else who prays to Him. You don't have to go to church for him to hear you." The three of them all laughed. "I think it's time for all of us to examine our lives. I hug my kids more now since this thing with Rebecca."

"That's great Louie, hang in there, we're all in this together. Your brothers all care about you."

"Thanks Richie, you do the same," Louie replied, as he gave Bobby and Richie each a big hug.

The high-pitched sound of clanking glass filled the room. Captain Bill Shields was standing on a chair in the center of the room banging a spoon against his empty glass. "Attention everyone, may I have your attention please. I want to take this opportunity to thank all of you for coming tonight. I hope you've had as good a time as I have. As has been our tradition in the past, it's time to thank our host and hostess for their great hospitality once again. Lucille, Anthony, Annemarie, come here please." Everyone began to applaud as the Margulos made their way to the center of the room. Lieutenant Farley held up his glass and began to speak. "A toast to Anthony, Lucille, and Annemarie. This Christmas party has become a tradition all of us look forward to all year long. Like always, you didn't disappoint us. We are honored that you go out of your way, and we look forward to next year's party." The guests began to applaud, and Anthony pulled Lucille and Annemarie close to him.

Vinny Amarosa and Willie Johnson then approached the Margulos and gave each of them a gift box. "As the senior men of Ladder 179 and Engine 200, it is our privilege to present you with these gifts. We hope you enjoy them. You always go out of your way for us, and the men just wanted to say thank you. Anything else you want to add Willie?"

"Yes Vinny...just that in all my years of being a firefighter, I have never met a better bunch of guys than all of you in this room. I'm proud to call each of you brother. And to the Margulo family, thank you for being a part of our firehouse family. Go ahead now, open your gifts, I can't wait to see what we got you." This brought a big laugh from the crowd, as they all got closer for a better look.

One by one Lucille, Anthony, and Annemarie opened their gifts. They each received a navy blue sweatshirt with the logo of Ladder 179 and Engine 200 on the front, and a red, white and blue FDNY flag logo on the back. They also received a wooden maltese cross plaque. Each cross had a small gold plate with an inscription that read, "On behalf of the members of Ladder 179 and Engine 200, you have been appointed honorary members of the FDNY, and our companies. Thank you for your continued kindness and support."

Anthony Margulo wiped back a tear as he read the plaque. Lucille smiled, and Annemarie blushed. After gaining his composure, Anthony decided to say a few words. "As you know, this building is the only house I have ever lived in. My parents came to this country as poor immigrants. My dad built this restaurant with his bare hands. He came here for a better life, a better opportunity. Pop, I thank you for what you did for me," Anthony said as he looked upward. "I wish you and mom could still be with us today, to see how rich my family has become. Rich, not in money, but in the friendships our family shares with all these fine men and their families. We thank you for protecting us, and the whole neighborhood. If my daughter Annemarie comes to her senses about Ralphie over here, we will truly be a family."

Laughter and a loud applause filled the restaurant. Annemarie felt like she wanted to go crawl under a table. A few of the guys pushed Ralphie and Annemarie together and wanted them to dance. By the end of the night every person in the room felt a common bond. It was a bond of friendship and family that men in the fire service all share.

As the night ended, Ralphie and Annemarie had even made a date for Sunday night. Yes, even though their worlds would change dramatically in the next year, neither of them knew of the events that lie ahead. A new relationship brings a new beginning that each would share. Their lives, and the lives of everyone in this room were connected. As they left the party, each of them looked forward to next year's Christmas party. Little did anyone know, that this would be the last time each of them would be together as a group.

CHAPTER 5

January 11, 2001

The dog days of winter were upon New York. The Christmas trees, decorations, and lights were all taken down and packed away for another time and place. Each January, the city was transformed from bright and festive, to a dark gray cold. Hopefully, spring would return in a few months and bring a new beginning.

Instead of looking forward to spring training and baseball, New Yorkers still were focused on football season. The New York Giants were on their way to the Super Bowl. It was ten years since they were in the big game, but it seemed like an eternity. Midway through the season it looked like they might not even qualify for the post season. The team rallied behind their coach and was now one win away from the big game.

The football fans at the Palace were split right down the middle. Half rooted for the hometown Giants, while the other half were diehard Jets fans. The men had just gotten back from a run when the alarm bells started to ring. Bobby York was on house-watch and yelled the address over the firehouse intercom. "Auto accident with aided, extrication needed, corner of Henry and Carol Streets. Engine and Ladder go."

Each man jumped on the rigs and geared up. Within a few short minutes they would arrive at the scene. Ladder 179 carried a portable generator and a Hurst Jaws of Life. Each man assigned to 179 was qualified as a Hurst Tool operator. They each were assigned on a rotating basis to operate the tool. Tonight was Joey Donovan's turn. The men in the Engine Company were there in case a fire ignited from any spilled fuel from the accident.

The units arrived to find a late model sports car wrapped around the light pole on the corner. There were no other cars involved. Inside the car was a young man laughing very loudly. The glowing lights and screeching sirens filling the neighborhood amused him. His forehead had a gash that would require a number of stitches, but it didn't matter to him. As blood dripped from the open wound, the man laughed even louder.

Every policeman and fireman at the scene knew from past experience that this man had to be intoxicated. Why else would he be laughing after a head on collision with a light pole? As Joey Donovan approached with the Jaws of Life, Bobby Giordano and Louie Ludwig worked on the car door with an axe and halligan tool. They made enough of an opening for Joey to insert the spreader tip, and pry the passenger door open. Vinny Amarosa had already stabilized the car with wood blocks. Joey now changed the tips of the tool and began to make four cuts in the car roof. To the onlookers, it looked like Joey was taking the car apart with a huge can opener. He made two cuts where the car roof met the front posts, and two more cuts in the roof right behind the front side windows. Bobby and Vinny now pulled back the roof and folded it backwards. In a few short minutes the car had become a convertible.

The F.D.N.Y. paramedics now went to work removing the man from what was left of his vehicle. In addition to the wound in his forehead, he had suffered a fractured right ankle and leg. The force of the impact drove his foot back into his leg causing the bones to snap in half. In most cases, this would cause severe pain, but not this time. This man had so much to drink that he never felt a thing. Lucky for him he was wearing his seatbelt and the airbags inflated. When he looked down and saw his foot dangling in an odd angle he had never seen before, he finally passed out.

After arriving at Long Island College Hospital, a blood sample would be drawn in order for the Police to conduct a blood alcohol test. The man might not remember how the accident happened, but he was still responsible for his actions. Lucky for him, no one else was hurt this time. After sobering up, his laughing would turn to tears when he found out about the loss of his new car, and the charges he would face.

The car was towed away, and Jim Lennon pulled the portable booster line that was mounted on top of Engine 200. He would wash down the intersection of any glass and debris. Because of the cold weather, Captain Shields ordered Ralphie to throw down shovels of sand. The last thing anyone wanted was for the water to freeze, and turn the intersection into a sheet of ice. Jimmy Daly pushed the broken glass and metal to the curb, and the men climbed into their rigs for the ride back to the palace. As the temperature dropped, they all hoped the neighborhood would stay quiet for the night.

The rigs pulled up parallel to the firehouse and the men jumped out of the cab. Engine 200 and Ladder 179 then backed up in unison to the sound of their beeping backup alarms. The chauffeurs guided the tires right down the center of the yellow lines painted on the gray firehouse floor. When the back wheels hit the rubber stops, the engines were cut and the airbrakes hissed their last breath. The men climbed out of their bunker gear, and left it near their respective riding positions. Captain Shields and Lieutenant Farley would return to their office to fill out the department paperwork. Ralphie Chiarello jumped on top of Engine 200 to refill the water tank from the garden hose that hung from the ceiling. As the firehouse probie, this would remain his job until a new probie came along. When he was done, he returned to the day room with to join others.

The talk around the firehouse these days rotated around football, the city investigation into Rebecca's death, and our new President. The investigators exonerated the Fire and Police Departments of any wrongdoing. The departments had won the battle, but lost the war. Rebecca was still gone, and nothing could bring her back. The blame clearly lied with her foster parents. Their television and stereo were worth more to them than Rebecca. Maybe if she were one of their own, they would have felt different.

The Fire Department Union was very active too. With the start of the New Year, it was time for them to air their concerns. The major problem that faced them was field communications. Simply put, the new radios the city had purchased, did not work. Signals were lost, and urgent messages were not being heard. This problem became worse when the radios were being used in high-rise buildings, or underground in the subway system.

The subways in New York City are the tributaries that feed life into the skyscrapers. Without the subways, transportation would come to a halt, and the buildings would be empty voids of concrete and steel. Over three million people ride the subways on a daily basis. You can meet people from all different races and religions just by taking a short ride. For their fare, riders get a one-way trip. Everyone is treated the same. There are no first class seats.

While testing the radios a few months earlier, the emphasis had been put on quality and durability. In order to get the new radios in service quickly, it seemed the Department had moved too fast and the reliability factor was overlooked. The Union called for a recall of all the new radios that were in service until an adequate field test could be conducted by the manufacturer, and the department. As in any other large organization, the issue would get caught up in red tape. In the meantime, the radios would remain in service.

Ralphie entered the day room to find everyone either reading the newspaper or watching television. "Hey Chiarello, how's the love life these days," Jim Lennon shouted.

"Yeah probie, you still seeing Annemarie," Bobby York added as he refilled his mug with some freshly brewed coffee. Before he had a chance to reply, all eyes in the room were upon Ralphie. Tonight's entertainment would be at Ralphie's expense.

He smiled his sheepish smile, raised his eyebrows and laughed. "It's going good I guess."

"Don't give me going good Ralphie, what does that mean?"

Ralphie knew everyone was listening and was thinking of a smart reply when the Palace phone began to ring. Vinny Amarosa picked up the receiver and all of a sudden a huge smile came over his face. "Ralphie, there's no one here named Ralphie. What, did he tell you he was a fireman, aha, aha, ...yeah, well, he probably told you that so you would go out with him."

Ralphie started to turn red and begged Vinny to give him the phone. "Hey Vinny, come on now, enough, can I please have the phone."

The rest of the crew was hysterical watching Ralphie squirm. Vinny couldn't keep a straight face anymore and told the caller to hang on. "It's for you Ralphie boy, it's Annemarie."

Ralphie walked across the room to take the call. As Vinny handed the phone to him, the crew all got up from their seats and crowded in to hear the call. Before he said hello, Ralphie turned around and saw all his buddies crowding in. "Well, you gonna say hello or what kid?" Captain Shields chimed in. "Don't keep the lady waiting."

"Hello....yeah, hi Annemarie." Ralphie was very embarrassed and started whispering into the phone.

"We can't hear you kid, talk louder."

"Tell her you love her."

"Ask her if she has any good looking cousins for me."

All these things were being said out loud while Ralphie tried to have a conversation with Annemarie. All of a sudden Captain Shields grabbed the phone and started to speak. "Annemarie?

Yeah, Captain Shields here, listen, it's getting late and it's past Ralphie's bedtime, I'm sorry, but we have to tuck him in now. He didn't have a nap today and he's been quite cranky." All of the guys were now laughing uncontrollably. Ralphie stood there taking it all in. He knew the guys were only kidding. Being the brunt of the joke was a small price to pay for his acceptance.

"I'll give him back the phone to say goodnight. You take care Annemarie, and say hello to your folks for me."

"O.K. Captain, thanks, I will, you have a good night too. Stay safe." As Annemarie sat there she knew she was falling for Ralphie. She loved being around him and even envied the closeness that he shared with his coworkers. They were full of life. Why couldn't she have that same bond with the people she worked with? They came to work waiting for the day to end. Not Ralphie though. He looked forward to going to work. He knew that becoming a firefighter had changed his life. He believed in fate. He could have wound up in any firehouse in the city, but he was assigned to the Palace. This is where he was supposed to be. His life would forever be tied together with his brothers there, and with Annemarie. No, it was not a coincidence that he was assigned to Engine 200. It was part of God's big plan.

Richard Damante

During the next few months Ralphie would grow even closer to Annemarie and Joey. Joey would look to Ralphie as the dad he never knew. Joey would come home from school and run right over to the Palace if he knew Ralphie was working. He knew when he grew up he wanted to be just like Ralphie and the other firefighters. While most kids his age were playing video games, Joey was learning all about becoming a firefighter. The men had some old gear they even let him wear.

Many people think that firefighters are boys who never grew up. It really is just the opposite. Firefighters are men who not only grew up, but also have a love for life that most people never experience. As they age, they remain young at heart. Their love for life leads them to experience life in its fullest. Sure, they have fun, but they know the true meaning of life doesn't lie with how much money you make or how big a house you own. Life is about people and the lives you touch daily.

CHAPTER 6

February 11, 2001

Just like he had done for the last 20 years, Alan Jenkins arrived to work at 5:45 A.M. He lived by the belief that it was better to be fifteen minutes early, than fifteen minutes late. As he walked into the lobby of 1 World Trade Center, he began to get nostalgic. Just last night he and his wife Amy made the decision that he would retire on September 14th. Even though he was already eligible for retirement, the extra few months of income would come in handy.

As a retirement gift to themselves and their family, Alan and Amy had booked a Caribbean cruise. They would spend a week basking in the tropical sun surrounded by their children and grandchildren. It would be the best vacation any of them ever had.

After retiring from the New York City Police Department in 1981, Alan took the job working at the Information Desk of the World Trade Center. His job entailed being both a security guard, and helping people find their way through the various buildings that comprised the World Trade Center. While part of the NYPD, he was assigned to the 15th Precinct Detective Squad in lower Manhattan. He knew the downtown area very well. He had watched the buildings rise floor by floor while they were being built in the late 1960's and early 1970's. Many people thought the two narrow steel structures were an eyesore, but not Alan. Yes, they were taller than any other building in the area, but they also had a personality of their own.

Visitors were awed by their sheer magnitude. It wasn't until you were inside the building, that you felt their presence. On windy days the buildings would sway with the wind. It was designed that way to withstand the winds that would blow in from the bay during the blustery winter months. The buildings were also strong enough to withstand a direct hit by a 707 Jet, one of the largest planes at the time. They were an engineering marvel that couldn't be built in any other city of the world except New York.

The Twin Towers stood for America. They brought new life to a downtown area that was on the decline. Just like America was built on hopes and dreams, so were the towers. People from over 100 different countries worked in the World Trade Center. They represented people from all different walks of life, cultures, and religions. They were engineers, architects, janitors, chefs, stock- brokers, secretaries, and clerks. America was a melting pot, and so were the towers.

Alan settled in at the main information desk located in the large lobby of 1 World Trade Center. Over the years he got to know many of the workers whom he greeted each morning. Thousands of people would pass by everyday. He couldn't possibly know them all, but he had his favorites. They were more than faces. They were people. They had families and secrets just like Alan. They came there to earn a living.

As he unfolded the morning issue of the New York Post, the first of the daily workers began to arrive. Most of the people were usually in their offices by 9:00 A.M. From 9:00 A.M. until his shift ended at 3:00 P.M., Alan would be busy giving directions to the many visitors and tourists who would ride one of the 97 elevators up to the observation deck.

Alan knew the World Trade Center complex better than most of the other security guards he worked with. He knew the layout of each building, and which firms occupied the 220 floors of office space. Being an ex-police officer taught Alan valuable lessons. He knew how to size up a person when he first met them. He knew the signs to look for to locate trouble. He was a rock under pressure.

When the first World Trade Center bombing occurred back in 1993, Alan took part in the evacuation process. He helped many people to safety that cold and snowy February day. After it was over he felt anger toward those who could do such a horrible thing. Hatred might have won the battle that day, but it didn't win the war. There were injuries and even death, but the buildings still stood as a symbol of America, and of humanity. In the darkest of times, love for a fellow man shone brightly as civilians and rescue workers one by one sacrificed their own safety for total strangers.

Some of the people who survived that day in 1993 never returned to work. They believed by escaping death once, it would be hard to return. Others believed that it was only a matter of time before another attack would occur. The public knew little about al-Qaeda back then. Some companies actually moved their whole operation not only from the World Trade Center, but from Manhattan altogether. They moved to the peace and quiet of the Long Island or New Jersey suburbs. They felt safer there, feeling that if another attack was to occur, New York City was the prime target. They left in fear, but not Alan Jenkins.

Alan was more motivated now than ever before. He took it personally and vowed that no one would ever dictate how or where he lived or worked. Manhattan was his city, and he served it proudly for over 40 years. He loved New York and he loved the Towers. He knew them like the back of his own hand. They were a city within a city. They were self- sufficient. A person could arrive there for work in the morning and eat, shop, work, and never leave the buildings until it was time to catch the train home.

"Good morning Alan, how are you today?"

"I'm fine Annemarie, how's it going with you?"

A big smile came across Annemarie's face as she started to answer. "Things are real good, thanks for asking Alan."

"I knew it, you must be in love, I can tell, it shows in your smile these days."

"Really, oh my", Annemarie blushed.

"Yeah kid, I've raised two daughters of my own, I know what to look for," Alan chuckled. "What is he like? How long you been going together?"

"Well, it's happening really fast. His name is Ralphie, and he's a firefighter. My son has taken a real liking to him too. I just hope it works out, I'd hate to see him hurt."

"Good luck to you Annemarie, sounds like a good guy. I always said the next best man to a cop is a firefighter. Does he work here in the city?"

"No, he is over at Engine 200 in Brooklyn, over by my apartment. That's how we met. My parents really like him too."

"That means a lot. I know you and your family are real close. I got some good news myself. I'm giving my notice later on today. Finally going to take the plunge and retire."

"Congratulations Alan, we're going to miss you though. How soon are you leaving? When is your last day?"

"Not until September 14th. Figured I would work one more summer, save some more money, take the family on a nice vacation after that."

"Good for you Alan. You deserve it. I'm glad we'll still get to see you for a while. See you later."

"Yeah, you too. Have a good day Annemarie."

Annemarie walked past the information desk over to the elevator banks. She would ride two separate elevators to get up to her office on the 94th floor. As she rode alone in the elevator, her thoughts turned to her conversation with Alan. Was she really that in love that people knew it just by looking at her? Her life had changed and she was happy for it. Maybe Joey could someday have someone he could call dad.

Joey and Annemarie had a very close relationship. Being the only man in the house made Joey very protective of his mom. He usually was leery of any man that showed Annemarie attention, but not this time. He went out of his way to get the two of them together. Ralphie, Annemarie and Joey were starting to become a little family of their own. Joey loved his grandpa very much and no one could ever replace him, but Ralphie was quickly becoming Joey's hero.

The elevator came to a sudden stop. The bells rang and the doors opened. Annemarie unlocked the office doors and turned on the lights. She was the first one in once again. Her job these days had become very stressful. It was all about the bottom line. At the end of the day, millions of dollars were exchanged between accounts. Clients trusted her with their futures. She was personable and very intelligent. She would never take a chance with a client's investments that she wouldn't with her own money.

A few hours later, the building had come to life. It was estimated that 50,000 people came in and out of the doors on a daily basis. After lunch, Alan had a meeting with his supervisor and handed in his retirement notice. The two men felt both happy and sad at the same time. Alan was a worker anyone would hate to lose, but he had worked hard all his life, and it was time for him to move one. Sure, the people would miss him, but they would go on. The World Trade Center would get by without him. The buildings would still be standing long after Alan's time on earth ended. Life goes on independent of any one person. On September 17th everything in the buildings would be the same. The only difference would be a missing Alan Jenkins. People would arrive at work and earn a living, but someone else would be there to greet them. Yes, Alan knew he had made the right decision. He didn't feel it now, but he knew as the day of his retirement drew near, he would start to feel melancholy. It was only natural. Another chapter of his life would close, and a new one would begin. Every second, of every day, of every life, being woven together. No chance encounters, but dates with destiny.

Originally Alan and Amy had decided that his last day of work would be September 7th. They would leave on September 9th for the family cruise. The date was pushed back one week when the travel agent called them back with a better deal for the following week. They changed their original plans not knowing how the consequences of their decision would play out. A simple decision would change their lives forever, but none of them knew it this February day.

CHAPTER 7

March 11, 2001

Two months had passed and the radio problems were still the same. The union was frustrated, and so were the firefighters. The field test results were still the same, but the men were growing concerned. Did someone have to die before the problem was fixed?

It had been a few months since Richie or any of the other men had dreamed about Rebecca. The more they worked, and the more fires they responded to, the easier it was to forget. Spring training was in full swing, and the dream of another Subway series filled every baseball fan in the city.

Engine 200 and Ladder 179 had responded to the Court Street Subway station a few hours earlier and were still at the scene. A passenger had slipped when entering the Number 2 Manhattan bound IRT. She was now wedged in between the train and the concrete platform. What made the job even harder was her size and girth. The woman weighed over 200 pounds, and she was jammed in good. There was little room for the men to maneuver themselves, and the woman.

Captain Shields had radioed for the power to the third rail to be shut down as soon as the men arrived. This was standard operating procedure while working on or near the tracks. The radio message was never heard though, but the men did not know it. They knew better than to go anywhere near the third rail, but if the train moved, it could cost the woman her life. The call for more equipment and manpower was not heard either. Vinny Amarosa ran up the steps to the street and resent the message. Finally, the message was heard. Power was cut, and other units were on the way. Rescue Company 2 got there a few minutes later and took over the overall rescue operations.

There are over 200 Engine and Ladder Companies in the FDNY, but only five Rescue Companies. These five companies are spread out throughout the five city boroughs. Rescue 1 is located in Manhattan, Rescue 2 Brooklyn, Rescue 3 the

Bronx, Rescue 4 Queens, and Rescue 5 in Staten Island.

The Rescue Companies are made up of elite firefighters and officers. Each member is hand picked based upon their experience, education, and any special training they have received. They respond to all multiple alarm fires, and any call where the special equipment they carry is needed. If they can't get the job done, no one can. The Ladder and Engine companies like to joke about the Rescue guys all being prima donnas, but they respect the jobs they perform. To be asked to join a Rescue Company means you are the best of the best. Everything about the Rescue Companies is different than the other companies, even their rigs.

The Rescue rig is a large box truck with many doors and compartments to carry all the special tools they use. The early Rescue men took a lot of ribbing. Their rigs looked like bread delivery trucks. Over the years, as the need to carry more equipment grew, so did the size of the rigs. No one mistook a Rescue Company rig for a bread delivery truck anymore.

The job of a Rescue Company officer was one of the toughest jobs in the Department. They needed to know everything about firefighting their counterparts in the Ladder and Engine companies knew, and even more. They drilled their men daily on building collapses; high-rise rescues, water rescues, and the tools that they needed to use. A special extrication tool might sit on the rig for years without ever being used once. When the time came that it was needed, the men had to know how to use it. It was a demanding job, but one each and every member of the Rescue Company was proud of. They may be cocky at times, but they could be. They earned their respect by the many unit and individual citations they received throughout the years. A medal day ceremony never went by without a Rescue Company member or Unit being recognized for an outstanding job.

As Richie and the other members of Ladder 179 and Engine 200 attended to the trapped woman, the men of Rescue 2 arrived at the scene. They immediately looked over the situation and started to work. They brought with them the heavy-duty air bags that would be used to push the train away from the trapped woman. Before the train could be moved, they had to be sure power was cut to the tracks in both directions. Once that was done, cribbing would be placed to keep the subway car stable, and then the men would crawl underneath the train to check for any other injuries to the victim.

Her name was Mary Obradors. She was a Hispanic woman in her early thirties. She spoke little English, but enough to know that the rescue workers were there to help her. She kept calm throughout the whole ordeal, even though the pain was intense. The longer she was stuck her breathing became heavier as she gasped for air. The pressure of the train and the platform against her chest was making breathing difficult as time went by. Paramedics had already administered oxygen to her to keep her from going into arrest.

Freddie Callaghan and Billy Stein from Rescue 2 had by now crawled under the train and gotten to the lower half of Mary's body. There appeared to be no trauma or broken bones. All that needed to be done, was to support her, and push the train away from the platform. The rescuers on top would tie a rope around her waist to keep her from sliding further down once the train was pushed away.

As the airbags were put in place, two New York City transit cops pushed the crowd of onlookers back. Just like the firefighters in New York City, the civilians see a lot in their lives too. Many of the riders who were removed from the train didn't want to miss out on this early afternoon excitement.

Richard Damante

Lieutenant Roger McBride was on duty today and gave the orders to start inflating the airbags. The airbags themselves were heavy square balloons made out of reinforced synthetics that could stand thousands of pounds of pressure. They could lift cars or trucks, and even subway trains right off the ground. Once a safe area was secured, and Mary was ready, the bags began to inflate. Slowly, the subway train began to move. The inflation would continue at a slow pace. This was done to make sure the pressure would not cause the bags to burst. The bags were built to withstand high loads, but in the game of life and death, it was better to be safe than sorry.

Usually a few inches of space was all that was needed to free a trapped victim, but not this time. Because of her size, it would take more than that. Finally, her body began to slip. The men pulled on the rope and lifted her to safety. The paramedics then placed her in a stokes basket. It took four men to carry the basket up the stairs and into the waiting ambulance. If everything checked out at the hospital, Mary might even be home in time for dinner.

The crews all picked up their equipment and the power was turned back on to the tracks. Many people would be late for their afternoon appointments today. They entered back into the train, and in a few minutes were on their way.

Such is the life of a subway rider. You never know what to expect. Once you think you've seen it all, something else happens to amaze you.

As the officers gave the signal to return to quarters, the men of Ladder 179, Engine 200 and Rescue 2 said their goodbyes, and gave their pats on the back for another job well done. The guys from the Palace knew they could have done the job by themselves if they had the right equipment onboard. Oh well, that's life. No one got hurt, and Mary would live another day to ride the subway. Maybe next time she would be more careful.

The rest of the day turned out to be rather uneventful. After dinner, Joey Donovan serenaded the men with his bagpipes. Joey was a piper in the FDNY Emerald Society Band since 1989. In six days he would be marching proudly down Fifth Avenue in the annual Saint Patrick's Day Parade.

The Emerald Society was synonymous with Saint Patrick's Day. This would be the fortieth straight year they would proudly wear the colors of the FDNY down the Fifth Avenue parade route. The Emerald Society was organized in 1961. Joey's uncle was an original member of the band. On holidays the Donovan family would all gather at Grandma Donovan's to listen to him play the pipes. Joey first picked up the bagpipes when he was 15 years old. Thirty- five years later he still had the passion to play, and was one of the lead pipers in the band. He considered it an honor whenever the band was called to play at a firefighters funeral or memorial service.

Saint Patrick's day would also be Joey's 51st birthday. He was a big man, standing six foot seven inches tall. The men at the Palace always kidded him about his size. They said he didn't need a ladder; he came equipped with his own. He was third generation FDNY. His grandfather and dad also served in ladder companies. The Donovan family was proud of their Irish heritage, and their 65 years of continued service to the city of New York.

"Hey Joey, play Amazing Grace for me will you," Richie pleaded. Joey winked and pressed the bellows with his elbow as the first high-pitched notes of Amazing Grace filled the Palace. Every man on duty stopped what he was doing just to listen. They all knew the words. Some sang out loud, others whispered or hummed. The song had a special meaning to each and every one of them. To some, it represented a new beginning, to others, an end. It was played at every funeral of every firefighter. To Richie, the song was life itself. The closer his walk with God, the more it meant to him. The tears it brought to his eyes were not tears of sorrow, but of joy.

"Amazing Grace, how sweet the sound, that saved a wretch like me..." As he sang these words it all came back. How God played a major role in his life and his family's life. He wished each of his brothers here at the Palace felt the same way he did, but he knew it wasn't the case. They all believed in God. They were all good men, and by the very nature of their job did good deeds everyday. This wasn't enough though. To make their lives full, they had to ask God into their hearts. Maybe one day they would. Maybe one day Richie would be given the chance to show them the way. You're never too old, and it is never too late to change. In the meantime, Richie promised he would be an example by the way he lived his life and did his job. One life touches another until every action we do affects everyone we come in contact with each and every day.

CHAPTER 8

April 11, 2001

Carl Risland had just walked out of the conference room when his cell phone began to ring. "Hello, this is Carl."

"Hi honey...it's me," his wife Emily replied.

"Hey, how did the doctor's appointment go?"

"He said everything is fine. Gave me some vitamins to take. He said I'll need them now that it's me and the baby." There was a long pause before Carl answered. "Did you just say what I thought you said Emily? A baby?"

"That's right...you're going to be a daddy Carl." Emily was beaming from ear to ear when she told her husband the news. They had almost given up hope of ever having a child of their own.

Carl and Emily had been married since 1988. They both were adventurous, fun loving individuals. For the last ten years they had tried unsuccessfully to start a family of their own. It was hard for Emily to see all her sisters and friends with children of their own, but now she too would know what it was like to be a mom. In a few months she would put her business career on hold and start a more demanding career. A career with low pay, and long hours, but one that was more rewarding than all the rest. A career that would mold a life from its very beginning. Elan Executive Travel Services, located on the 58th floor of 1 World Trade Center would have to get by without their top sales representative. Maybe one day, after her child was grown she would return to work, but her immediate plans would be focused on the child she was expecting in December.

Carl Risland also worked at the World Trade Center. The couple met each other one evening back in 1986. They were both meeting dates for dinner at the Windows of the World Restaurant located atop the World Trade Center. Their dates were both late in arriving. While waiting, they struck up a conversation and found out they had a lot in common. Three weeks later they met again while waiting for an elevator. Carl knew this wasn't a chance encounter and asked Emily to join him for lunch. She gladly accepted, and two years later they were joined together as husband and wife.

Carl excitedly walked back into the meeting and announced the news. His co-workers all shook his hand and he was grinning from ear to ear. All his life he dreamed about one day being a dad. Carl was adopted at a very young age and never knew his biological parents. He told himself that when the time came, he would be the best dad he could be. What a great day it was. Not only did he find out about the baby today, but he also got the promotion he was waiting for. The extra money would come in handy. Emily would continue to work until mid October, but then the bills would be on his shoulders. It was perfect timing.

Emily took the 10:05 Express train from Mineola to Penn Station, New York. Although she loved the city, she hated the daily commute. The Long Island Railroad wasn't so bad. She usually had a seat the whole way to Penn Station. It was the subway that got to her. The trains were always crowded with people pushing and shoving their way in like a can of sardines. It was only a fifteen-minute ride from Penn Station to downtown Manhattan, but it usually was the most stressful part of her day. She would miss her job, her office, and the city. The subway was a different story.

The whole commute into the city, she thought about how happy her husband sounded on the telephone. She knew he would be a great dad to their baby. They both had a lot of preparation ahead of them. They had just moved into their new home, and it needed work. Some of the plans would now be put on hold. The baby would be at the top of the list. The home office would be moved into the basement, and the nursery would take its place. It would be so much fun shopping for the furniture and picking out the colors. If she knew Carl like she thought she did, he would want to get started on the project right away.

When she arrived at her office, she broke the news of the upcoming blessed event. Her friends were just as excited as she was. They all loved Emily and knew how hard she and Carl had tried to start a family. In the back of their minds, they knew she would be leaving in a few months to give birth. They hoped she would return to work, but the ball was in her court.

Like Alan Jenkins, Emily would start a new chapter in her life. They both planned their futures and proceeded to get on with their lives. The one thing they didn't plan on, was the events taking place all across the world. Secret meetings were underway in Europe, the Middle East, and in the United States. Money was being transferred and hidden in bank accounts all over the world. Foreign students were enrolled in flight schools in Florida and Arizona. These students would blend into society and keep a low profile. They were loners who only associated with people just like themselves. They had no use for strangers, and made no friends. All of them lived a modest life so as not to bring light upon themselves. Their plan was underway. Some of them knew the mission, but not the date or time. In the meantime, life would go on as normal in New York, Boston, Florida, Washington D.C., and Arizona.

The great melting pot of the United States of America would be their disguise. Yes, America, land of the free, and home of the brave. Where people could be themselves in spite of their race or religion. America, the land of opportunity, and education. People from all over the world came here year after year seeking an education. All they needed was a student visa. It was easy to acquire, too easy as it turned out. The Statue of Liberty beckoned, "Give me your tired, your poor, your huddled masses yearning to breathe free." This phrase was inscribed on the base of the statue, but the world was now a different place. Instead of coming to America for work, education, or freedom, some chose to come to America to do her harm. Five months from this day, the world would watch in horror as their plan unfolded. Evil was lurking not in the shadows, but right out in the open.

They thrived on their hatred for America and our way of life. Their attack would be swift and far reaching. Their weapons would not be bombs or guns, but something no one ever would suspect. Our guard was down. The plan was in motion. The actions of these men would send tremors throughout the world. Once again, one life touching another, until every life, every moment intertwined together. History would repeat itself once again. Only the names and the faces would be different. Man against man. Good versus evil, and country against country.

CHAPTER 9

May 11, 2001

Spring filled the air as Little Leaguers, children, adults, and bicyclists were busy in the parks of New York. The winter had been a long cold one. Springtime was a time of renewal. A new beginning of life, as nature's colors changed from gray and brown to bright blues and greens. Homeowners were busy planting flowers and finishing up spring-cleaning just in time for the weekends Mothers Day celebration.

Alan Jenkins was at the Information Desk thinking about the party that was planned for Sunday at his daughter's house. How blessed he felt to have such a close-knit family. Many men and women in law enforcement allowed the job to eat away at them and their families, but not Alan Jenkins. His family is what mattered most in his life.

It was the same for Carl and Emily Risland. Their family was about to grow in five short months. The arrival of their first-born child would bring forth a change. They would trade their love of travel, for the love of another human being. Their freedom would be controlled by a fragile new life, one dependent on others to feed it, and to take care of it. It was a trade that Carl and Emily would gladly make.

Ralphie and Annemarie would spend Mothers Day at the family restaurant. Mothers Day was a busy day in the restaurant business, and Giovanni's Cucina Siciliana was no exception. If Ralphie wanted to be with Annemarie on Mothers Day, he would have to help out at the restaurant. He didn't mind. It was a small price to pay to be with the woman he loved more and more each day.

It was 8:15pm, and the men at the Palace were gathered around the television switching back and forth between the Met game, and the Yankee game. The NHL and NBA playoffs were in full swing, but none of the New York teams had a good year. Fans quickly lost interest when the home teams were out of post-season play.

Captain Pete Dolan popped his head in the day room and asked Richie to come with him to his office. Although fairly new to Ladder 179, Captain Dolan knew his men well. He was a short man standing only 5 feet 6 inches tall. What he lacked in stature, he made up for in his abilities. He was well respected throughout the FDNY, and had served in command positions in Brooklyn, Queens, and Manhattan. His men lovingly referred to him as Stretch Dolan.

Pete's dream was to one-day serve as a Battalion Chief. As the years passed, his dream began to slip away. If he were not promoted in the next few years, his days as a firefighter would soon come to an end.

Richie followed Captain Dolan into the cramped little office he shared with the other officers stationed at the Palace. "Have a seat Richie, I have some good news for you." Richie immediately sat down to hear what the Captain had to say. He had no idea what was coming. He had taken the Lieutenant test and hoped it may be news about that. "Richie, you're a good fireman," Captain Dolan blurted out, "A darn good one. You can watch my back in any fire and I'd feel safe. I've got a good friend at Rescue 4, in Queens, who has been asking about you. They'll be looking for a few new guys in a few months due to some retirements. They're watching you."

Richie sat there taking it all in. He was flattered that Rescue 4 was interested in him, but at the same time felt confused. Ladder 179 was his home. It was all he had ever known. It was an honor to be recruited by a Rescue Company, but his allegiance was to his brothers at the Palace. "I don't know what to say Captain, I'm speechless. When do they want me?"

"Not for awhile. Three, four, five months even. They were hoping you would at least come over and work some fill in tours the next few months. You can meet the guys and see how they operate."

"I guess I can do that, but what about the guys here. There are other good firemen right here. Are they interested in any of them?"

"Just you Richie. They know you've got some experience as a diver and they'll be losing one of theirs."

"O.K., I'll do it Captain, but I need time to think about this. I don't feel right leaving this place."

"I know what you mean Richie. The crews here are very close, but this may be the opportunity of a lifetime for you. You'll be busier than you've ever been, but its very rewarding. I served in Rescue 4 for five years before becoming an officer. I wouldn't trade those five years for anything in the world. If you decide to leave, the guys will understand. They may razz you for awhile, but don't sweat it kid."

"Thanks Captain. I appreciate you looking out for me. Hey, any word on your promotion yet?"

"No, not yet Richie, it may be awhile. I'm on the list. I'm hoping it happens soon though. I ain't no spring chicken anymore." The two men laughed and Richie got up and shook Stretch Dolan's hand. He started walking out of the office and paused. "Captain, what you said before, about me covering your back, the feelings mutual. I know when you give us an order, you wouldn't make us do something you weren't willing to do yourself." The Captain nodded and then went back to filling out his paperwork.

Instead of returning to the day room, Richie walked to the front of the firehouse. He pressed the yellow button on the wall, and the large red bay door slowly opened upward. It was a beautiful night. There were people sitting on the sidewalk in front of their houses chatting with their neighbors. Children were playing jump rope, as others skateboarded down the street between the parked cars. The cars were parked one behind the other. Parking was always hard to find in this neighborhood. Ever since the property values skyrocketed in the 1980's, there were no more vacant lots. The owners found out they made more money selling their property to builders, than renting it out as parking spaces.

The glow of the Manhattan skyline grew brighter as the night sky darkened. New York city was located right across the river, just a short ride away on the other side of the Brooklyn Bridge. It was close in distance, but worlds apart in everything else compared to this Brooklyn neighborhood.

Lower Manhattan was the world's financial district. It was home to the stock exchanges, and the commodity exchange. Millions of dollars exchanged hands on an hourly basis throughout the day. From Monday through Friday her streets were crowded with workers, tourists, and sidewalk vendors. The aroma of freshly cooked food filled the air. It seemed like there was a pushcart on every corner selling food of all different nationalities. Hot Dogs, sausages, knishes, and gyros satisfied the cravings of many New Yorkers on the go. These people seemed to milk every minute of every day. It was said true New Yorkers walked in straight lines, moving fast and eager to get to where they were going. You could tell the natives from the tourists just by the way they walked. The tourists were the ones who walked slowly, with their heads tilted back, looking up at the skyscrapers.

Even though Richie was a native New Yorker, every now and then he would catch himself doing the same thing. What an awesome city. It had been months since he had crossed the river into Manhattan. The majority of his time was spent either in Brooklyn at the Palace, or at home on Long Island. As a boy he had watched the city grow. He was amazed at how tall the buildings really were. He watched the Verrazano Bridge, the World Trade Center, and the Citicorp building all go up during his childhood. When they ran out of real estate to build on, they just built them taller and taller.

The city was an engineering marvel unto itself. As the population grew, so did the need for roads, bridges, tunnels, and the massive glass and steel structures that housed thousands of offices. Yes, man truly was a brilliant creature, but where did his brilliance come from? The desire to learn was a God given instinct.

"Hey Richie, what are you doing out here by yourself," Ralphie shouted as he walked up behind him.

"Just taking in the beauty of the city. You ever just sit back and ask yourself how? Why? Where did this all come from?"

"Not really, I guess being born and raised here its no big deal. I kind of take it all for granted, but I see what you mean."

"Ralphie, look how big the city is. How tall the Twin Towers are. Then look at the sky and the stars. It makes me think how small we really are compared to everything in the heavens."

"Ah...you're just getting old and philosophical on me," Ralphie laughed.

"No, think about it. What is your purpose here Ralphie? We all have a purpose to our lives. No life is meaningless or more important than any other. You'll learn someday what I mean Ralphie. The longer you stay on this job, you'll find out."

"Geez, I was just coming out here to say hello. Next thing you know I'm talking to Socrates himself, the great philosopher." Richie put his arm on Ralphie's shoulder and the two men walked back inside the Palace.

At half past midnight, the alarm bells and the voice of the dispatcher broke the silence of the night. The men slid down the brass poles from their second story bunkroom, to the apparatus floor below. They were called to the dock area of the Brooklyn Navy yard for an odor of gas. The first due units responded and were quickly met with a single large orange and yellow flame shooting hundreds of feet in the air. An old propane tank used by the dock- workers was the culprit. The valve had burst off, and the flames rushed out.

The men knew there was no way to extinguish a propane fire. The only way to stop the flame was to block its source. The options were either to let it burn itself out, or close the valve. Since the valve was broken off, the propane would be allowed to burn freely until there was none left in the tank.

Engine 200 would wet down the large propane tank to keep it cool. Ladder 179 set up the ladder pipe to place a wall of water between the tank and its nearest exposure. If the old warehouse caught fire, it would be a long night for everyone. How long the propane would burn was anyone's guess. It would either be another long night watching the sun rise over the eastern horizon, or pack up and go home in a few hours. Luckily for the firefighters, the tank was not full. The men would get to pick up and go back to their stations in a little over an hour. Thank God for little favors. As the men climbed on the rigs to go home, Captain Dolan and Captain Shields gave the 10-2 signal to return to their quarters. Captain Shields keyed his radio microphone and whispered, "Hey Stretch, someone's watching over us tonight."

"You got that right Shields, lets hope that guardian angel never quits his job. As a matter of fact, I think I see him lying down in your hose-bed right now." With that last remark, the crews returned to the Palace, and all was safe in Brooklyn Heights for the rest of the night.

CHAPTER 10

JUNE 11, 2001

It was 80 degrees and the sky was filled with sunshine as summer was on the way. A few weeks earlier Memorial Day marked the unofficial first weekend of the summer season. Pools opened, and backyard barbeques were now in full swing. In another two weeks, schools would be let out for summer vacation.

It was 6:00pm and Richie, Ralphie, and Louie Ludwig were all stuck in traffic on the Belt Parkway. The three men had started carpooling to the Palace a few months earlier. They all lived within a few miles of each other on the south shore of Long Island. Since Richie had the largest car, he usually did the driving while the others paid for the gas.

Richard Damante

The three men had just finished working the day tour at the Palace. The commute to and from work brought these three men even closer. They knew everything about each other and their families. Their discussions weren't just small talk. They were meaningful and each man was there to encourage the others. Today's topics were about their past failures, and the fears each of them carried within themselves. Their fears did not lay in dying, but in living, and living a meaningful life.

"God doesn't give you a dream to waste it Ralphie."

"I know Richie, I'm just afraid. What if she says no?"

Ralphie had just told Richie and Louie he planned to ask Annemarie to marry him. He knew he loved her and she loved him, but it was a very big step to take.

"Don't let your fear get in your way. You'll regret it the rest of your life. You know she's gonna say yes. She's crazy about you Ralphie."

"Louie, I know, but it's just not Annemarie and me. She has Joey to think about too."

"Is that what you're worried about. Let me tell you something. That kid looks up to you. All the time he spends with us at the firehouse, trust me, you're in. Don't worry about Joey. Annemarie knows how much Joey loves you too."

"Yeah, I know Louie, you're right."

"So when is the big day? When are you going to pop the question," Richie chimed in.

"This weekend. I'm meeting her at work on Friday night and taking her to dinner at Windows of the World. I figured it would be harder for her to say no in a setting like that."

"You know, I've lived in New York all my life and I've only been in the Trade Center twice. My mom and dad took me there when I was a kid, and then I went again in the '93 bombing."

"Don't feel so bad Louie, I haven't been there too many times either. I keep telling myself when I retire I'll have all the time in the world to sightsee and do all those things I have on my to do list. When I get home I'll have to add another item to that list. You just gave me an idea. I'll have to take Jane there on our anniversary in September."

"I can't believe you guys. You have to start living, doing more things. Enjoy life while you can."

"It's called marriage Ralphie," Louie joined in, "wife, kids, house payments. They all get the best of you sometimes. You sure you really want to get married?" The three men laughed and continued in their conversation.

"I wouldn't trade my life for anything. I'm not the richest man in the world, but I consider myself a success. Yeah, I've failed at times, we all have, but I don't dwell on it. It's all a learning experience."

"Hey Richie, how do you do it? What's the secret?"

"It's no secret Ralphie, it's called faith. I would be lost without it."

"Well I've got faith too Richie, but not like you, why?"

"It's up to you Louie, to take it to the next level. It's your choice. If you want it bad enough, ask for it. Pray about it."

"I know, I know, that's what my wife keeps telling me."

"Well listen to her, she knows what she's talking about."

All people at one time in their lives seek answers to life's mysteries. It is easy to believe in things you can see, smell and touch. Faith is believing in what you think is right regardless of the popular opinion. Richie, Louie, and Ralphie all shared a belief in what was right, and wrong. They all believed in God and in Jesus Christ His Son. Their faith was tested every day of their lives. It was easier to talk to their brothers at the Palace about the Yankees, Giants, or Knicks, than it was about God. Their belief lied in a better life than the one here on earth. This life was promised to them in the gospels of Matthew, Mark, Luke and John. A life so different than the one here on earth, it was indescribable.

Instead of running from his fears, Ralphie would rely on his faith. He would expect the best, and not the worst. In five days he would get down on his knees in the middle of a busy restaurant, and ask the woman he loved to marry him. Deep down he knew she would say yes. The ring was already purchased, and the reservations made. All that was left to do was the asking.

After dropping off Ralphie and Louie, Richie was left alone with his thoughts. He had worked a few shifts the last month down at Rescue 4. They were a great bunch of guys and made him feel welcomed there. It felt good to be wanted by an elite company, but it wasn't Ladder 179. Ladder 179 was his home, and it would stay that way unless he was promoted to Lieutenant. What mattered most to him were not the accolades that would come to him by being a part of Rescue 4. What mattered the most to him were his faith, family, and friends.

Later that same evening he made up his mind. He appreciated the opportunity but Ladder 179 was where his heart was. Jane agreed with his decision. She knew it was hard to pass up such a great opportunity, but felt like Richie made the right decision. If and when he became Lieutenant, they would have to go through the whole process once again. It would be at least another year until that decision would have to be made.

Back at the Risland residence, Carl had just finished painting the nursery. Carl and Emily had never been happier in their lives. Things were falling into place. Carl enjoyed his new position at work, and Emily loved being pregnant. On Friday, the Rislands would leave on a quiet vacation to upstate New York. They had rented a cabin on Lake George, and looked forward to the peace and tranquility away from work and the city. It would be the last vacation the two of them would enjoy before the arrival of their baby.

Alan and Amy Jenkins were now counting the days until retirement. In just three short months their careers would be behind them. They had each worked hard over the years to support their family. Now they would reap the rewards of all their hard work. Alan almost moved his retirement date up one month to August, but could not just let go that soon. Like Ralphie, he had fears, but his was of the unknown. What would retirement bring? Would he be bored? Would he grow old? He promised himself he would remain active and enjoy everyday he spent here on earth. On the top of his list was spending more time with Amy.

Before she went to bed, Annemarie said good night to Joey, and called Ralphie at home. The plans were made for dinner Friday night. Ralphie would pick her up at her office at 5:00pm. He told her it would be a special night full of surprises. She immediately became curious and begged Ralphie to tell her where they were going. Ralphie just laughed and said, "You'll just have to wait till Friday."

Annemarie was anxious in her own way. She thought Friday night would be the night Ralphie asked her to marry him. Of course she would say yes, but she still had worries. She was older than

Ralphie and already had a son of her own. She knew this didn't matter to Ralphie now, but would it make a difference down the road? Even though she knew the answer, her previous marriage caused her to be insecure about herself. She was a beautiful successful woman, but when she looked in the mirror, all she saw was Annemarie from Brooklyn, whose husband had abandoned her and her child. Could anyone really love her? All her self-doubts passed before her. The only way to confront her fears would be to jump right in with both feet. She realized the only way to feel content was by not containing her emotions. She would share her life with Ralphie and Joey, and unlock the love she had kept inside for years. Her failed marriage was an event. It would not be who she was the rest of her life.

CHAPTER 11

JULY 11, 2001

"So, you're a New York City fireman I see," the man behind the counter said to Richie as he handed him his dry cleaning.

"Yeah, that's right."

"How long have you been on the job?"

"This is my fifteenth year now."

"My brother in law is on the job too, Engine 10 in Manhattan, right across from the Trade Center."

"I'm in Brooklyn, Ladder 179, been there my whole career."

Richard Damante

"I'm an old truckie myself, Scotty Barnes, nice to meet you."

The man stuck out his hand and offered it to Richie.

"Nice meeting you too, I'm Richie Demarco."

"I'm also the ex-chief of the Volunteer Fire Department here in town. I've been to my share of fires too, but not like you I'm sure."

"Yeah, I've seen a lot over the years. More than I wish to remember, that's for sure. How much do I owe you for the cleaning?"

"Don't insult me Richie, it's on me. It's a gift, one fireman to another."

"Oh, you don't have to do that, but I appreciate it."

"Hey, no problem, I made sure we did a good job. I even shined the buttons myself. I'm guessing here, but I figured you wore it to the funerals last month."

"Unfortunately, yeah, you're right. It was a hard time for all of us. I got to know the guys from Rescue 4. I worked some tours there lately. Good men, all of them. It's been a real hard time for all of us."

"I knew the guy from Rockaway, great guy. I can't believe he is gone."

On Father's Day three FDNY firefighters perished in a blaze intentionally set by some kids. It was another tragic event that could have been prevented. A hardware store in Astoria, Queens was where it all took place. It was the first multiple firefighter fatality in years. Richie was on duty that day when the house radio at the Palace banged out the dreaded signal 5-5-5-5 for a line of duty death. It was a shock to all the guys. It really hit home with Richie since he recently got to know one of the men from working with him down at Rescue 4. One firefighter death was a lot to handle, but three all at once was unthinkable. Some of the men wept. Richie said a prayer for the men and their families. What went wrong? How could three men perish in the same fire? This event set off a chain of events that would have the FDNY being tested like no other time in history.

Over 300 firefighters from 75 companies responded to the five- alarm fire. It took them 12 hours to control the blaze. Two of the men from Ladder 163 were ventilating the front of the building when the façade collapsed on top of them. The other firefighter was assigned to Rescue 4. He was on the ground level of the store when the floor caved in and sent him tumbling into the basement inferno. He remained in radio contact for a while, but it took over four hours for the crews to find him. Because of the age of the building there were no sprinklers in the basement. This caused the fire to burn out of control and for the floor to cave in.

That day would forever be remembered by the eight children left fatherless - as the day their dads became heroes. The boys who set the fire were juveniles and could not be prosecuted as adults. In an unlikely turn of events, the family of one of the boys would bring a lawsuit against the Hardware Store for the injuries their son sustained while setting the fire. Once again, it was someone else's fault.

Since the FDNY was first formed in 1865 there had been 770 line-of-duty fatalities. In one day this number jumped to 773. It was a sad day that affected everyone associated with the Department. The navy blue Class A uniforms would be taken out of the closet and worn to the funerals. The flag at each firehouse across the city would fly at half- mast, and the black and purple bunting would be hung across the front of each FDNY firehouse.

People die in fires regardless of their age or occupation, firemen included. Even though they wear protective clothing and breathing apparatus it does not make them invincible. Three senseless deaths caused by some kids playing with matches once again. When would they learn?

The Mayor and the Fire Commissioner would attend the funerals. The Emerald Society Bagpipe band would be there also. These men had to put aside their emotions and play with a stone cold face. It was their duty to play at every funeral, and each of them considered it an honor. Amazing Grace would once again bring tears to the faces of the mourners. One of the local newspapers ran an editorial cartoon that showed the three firefighters who perished, approaching the gates of heaven. There was a sign that read "welcome home heroes." The editorial read, "Don't be afraid, those are clouds, not smoke." This cartoon hung on the bulletin board at the Palace. It was a reminder of their fallen brothers, and at the same time provided some comfort in this tragic event. These three men would now have nothing to fear.

Annemarie took the news very hard. She never really thought of the consequences of Ralphie's occupation until confronted with a firefighter's funeral for the very first time. She accompanied Ralphie to two of the funerals. She saw grown men crying for someone that most of them didn't even know personally. They lost a brother in arms, one of their own who answered the call to duty one last time.

She knew she made the right decision when she accepted the engagement ring from Ralphie, but what if this happened to Ralphie. She would once again be alone. She couldn't even bear to think about it. She had to remind herself not to let her fears dictate her life. The love she and Ralphie shared was real, and she would not be denied.

Ralphie spent more time with Annemarie these days. They were busy with the wedding plans, and it gave them both a reprieve from thinking about the Father's Day tragedy. They had set a date for the wedding to be held on Valentines Day 2002. They wanted the reception to be at Giovanni's, but due to the large number of family and friends they would be inviting, they had to find another option. They settled on a catering hall in Brooklyn, which was not too far from the neighborhood.

The guest list would include all the guys from the Palace and their wives. Annemarie would be walked down the aisle escorted by both her father and her son Joey. The honeymoon would be spent on a beach in Cancun, Mexico.

When Ralphie returned to the Palace for the night tour later on that day, the men had a surprise waiting for him in front of his locker. There, in a small box was an eight-week old Dalmatian puppy. They told Ralphie the puppy was an engagement present, but they would love to keep the dog at the firehouse. They even named the puppy Ralphie Junior, but decided they would just call him Junior.

Willy Johnson said the puppy even looked like Ralphie since both of them were still wet behind the ears. Junior quickly became the firehouse mascot. It was Ralphie's job to feed him and clean up after him. Like all Dalmatian puppies, he was a ball of pure white wrinkly skin with large paws and numerous black spots. He loved the attention the men gave to him, and quickly had learned how to get what he wanted from each of them. In return, he gave them all his unconditional love. No strings attached. He would live the role of the devoted firehouse dog, and mans' best friend.

Eventually, his picture would be hung on the wall as every other member of Ladder 179 and Engine 200. His name would be written in the permanent log of the Palace. He was more than just some dog. After the Father's Day fire, he became a comforter to the men. He took their minds off of everything bad that happened in their lives.

Richard Damante

His home was Engine 200 and Ladder 179. No life more important than the others. Each one affecting the others they touched, including the life of Ralphie Junior.

CHAPTER 12

AUGUST 11, 2001

"I don't know Jane, I've had this funny feeling for awhile now. First Rebecca, then the Father's Day fire, I feel like God is preparing us for something big. I keep praying. I pray for my family, the guys down at the firehouse. I know God has a plan for all of us. I ask Him to show me what it is I'm supposed to do for Him. I want Him to use me any way He can. I'm just not getting any answers."

"Richie, just keep praying. You know what Pastor Jim always says; our time is not God's time. He'll show you what it is when He is ready."

"I know Jane. I just get so anxious. I've had so many questions the past year."

"It's been hard on you. I understand, but don't lose your faith, not now. When things seem unbearable, that's when we learn Richie, hang in there." Richie walked over and embraced Jane. He kissed her and told her how much he loved her. Death was a part of living. Even with his faith, it wasn't easy. He thought more about his family than ever before. What if he was the one who didn't come home one day? What would happen to his family? The thought of not being with them tore him apart, but he must move on. Like Ralphie, Annemarie, and many others, he must break the cycle of fear that was building up inside him.

Jane waved to him from the front porch as he drove away. They had lived in the same house since 1983. It wasn't just a house. Their love made it a home. They never thought they would ever be able to afford a house of their own, but they saved enough to put down on a small Cape Cod style house. They lived in the house by themselves for three years. It was more than enough room. After the birth of the twins, it did get crowded at times, but none of them ever thought about moving. You can move from a house, but you never move away from a home.

Over the years they made changes. They added a front porch, and a backyard deck. Finding people to help do the work was no problem. The guys at the Palace were always willing to lend a hand. Every year, Richie and Jane hosted a Fourth of July party. The party was cancelled this year due to the Father's Day tragedy. Yes, life did go on, but Richie just didn't feel right about it this year. He promised everyone that next year's party would be bigger and better than ever.

When Richie arrived at the Palace, he was greeted by an ever- growing Ralphie Junior. This dog seemed to grow overnight. He was well fed, and well taken care of. He was also a big hit with the neighborhood. The men would take him with them everywhere they went. His favorite seat was the passenger side window seat in the crew compartment of Engine 200. The guys in the Engine Company always started kidding the Ladder Company how smart the dog really was. Even Ralphie Junior knew that real firefighters were assigned to Engine Companies, and not Ladder Companies.

Today was Joey Donovan's first day back to work since being a player coach for the FDNY basketball team that competed in the World Police and Firefighter games. The department was proud of these men, as they took home the gold medal. Joey was a former college star who played at Saint John's University. He was passed over by every NBA team due to a serious knee injury he sustained his senior year. He always thought it was funny that he could pass the demanding physical of the FDNY, but the NBA said he was damaged goods. To Joey, being a firefighter was much more demanding than running up and down a basketball court ever was.

Joey walked into the day room and was given a standing ovation by everyone present. "Joey my boy, I can't believe it, you came back to us. How is the star hoops player doing", Jim Lennon asked.

"Yeah, I didn't think you would still hang out with us peons since they hung that gold medal around your neck," Jimmy Daly added.

"Don't listen to them, they're just jealous," Bobby York chimed in. "Welcome home, we missed you."

"Thanks guys, it's good to be back home."

"Hey Joey, we hardly missed you. We even replaced you with this dog." The firehouse erupted in laughter as Ralphie walked in with Ralphie Junior.

"Say hello to our new probie Joey." Lieutenant Farley waved over to Ralphie as he spoke, and the puppy went running over to Joey Donovan.

"You'll never guess what we named him."

"I can only imagine Richie."

"Well, when we first got him, we gave him to Ralphie as an engagement present. One night at dinner Captain Shields noticed how much Ralphie and the dog looked like each other, so we named him Ralphie Junior." Joey started to laugh as Richie continued on.

"Just call him Junior, he likes it better." The puppy jumped up on Joey and began to lick his face. In a matter of minutes he had won over the heart of another firefighter. This dog was smarter than anyone realized.

The crews then sat around the large kitchen tables and asked Joey all about his experience at the games. He enjoyed his time away, but it felt great to be back with the guys. They all asked to see his gold medal. After kidding him about being away for so long, they all admitted how proud they were of him and the team.

Right before lunch, it was time for the company drills. Both companies would be practicing roof rescues off the rear of the firehouse. They would take turns being lowered to the ground in the stokes basket. The Engine Company guys would be lowered first, and Ralphie would be the first one in the basket. They all climbed the interior stairs to the roof except Bobby Giordano and Vinny Amarosa. Bobby and Vinny stood by on the ground for the basket to be lowered. This drill was a standard drill at every firehouse in the city, but today it would be a little different than usual. They were all in on the twist except for Ralphie.

After strapping Ralphie in the basket, Lieutenant Farley gave the order to start lowering him down the side of the building. Once he was below the roofline some of the guys went inside to retrieve the 20 gallon steel pots that they had filled with soapy water. Vinny and Bobby were waiting down below with fire extinguishers waiting for Ralphie to get closer to them. They too had a big surprise waiting for him.

When he was about 10 feet from the ground, the rope suddenly stopped. Ralphie started to get a little nervous and finally realized something was up. He thought the guys were just going to leave him hanging there and walk away. O.K, he fell for another one of their jokes. Was he that gullible he thought to himself? "Alright guys, let me down, the jokes over, you got me again."

"Oh Ralphie, you're too smart for us. O.K. guys, let him down, he's on to us, let's go." Captain Shields gave the order to lower him again. This time, when Ralphie looked up to the roof, all he saw were the grinning faces looking down on him. He knew he was in trouble. All of a sudden, gallons of cold soapy water came raining down on him. They drenched him from head to toe. The men on the roof were hysterical as Ralphie lay there helplessly tied up and dangling from the roof. The more Ralphie yelled, the harder everyone laughed. Finally, they lowered him to the ground. "O.K. guys, let me out now, the jokes over."

"Oh no it isn't Ralphie, you've got soap all over you. You need to be rinsed off."

"Let me go Vinny...please."

"You should know by now not to beg kid." With this, Vinny and Bobby sprayed Ralphie with the water in each of their portable extinguishers. By this time everyone had come down from the roof just in time to see Ralphie lying there in the basket, soaking wet. Once again, by his tolerance, Ralphie took one step closer to becoming one of the guys.

"No hard feelings kid, you passed your initiation."

"Yeah, no hard feelings Captain." They all shook hands and patted Ralphie on the back.

"Hey Ralphie, look at the bright side, now you don't have to shower today."

"You should have seen the look on your face when the water started to fall on you."

"You really are gullible, that was the easiest prank we ever pulled on anyone."

"I told you he was still wet behind the ears." They all got in a parting shot and returned to the day room. Richie had already started preparing the lunch of the day. Nothing fancy, just fried chicken, mashed potatoes, and fresh corn on the cob. Ralphie even got to eat free today for being such a good sport. Who said there was no such thing as a free lunch?

....

Bill Vogler was just returning from lunch when he was called into a meeting by his supervisor. Bill was a claims adjuster with United Metro Insurance Services. He had worked for them for the last eight years. His coworkers, and his superiors alike, respected him. Bill loved his job, and he loved his new life even more.

In September of 1999 Bill married his childhood sweetheart. He had remained single all these years, and would think about Cathy often. When Bill went off to college, he lost track of Cathy. She married another man and broke Bill's heart. He never thought he could love another woman the way he loved Cathy. One night he decided to go to a singles dance at his church. He was regretting going, when all of a sudden he saw someone out of the corner of his eye. It was Cathy. They hadn't seen each other in years. He ran over to her and gave her a big hug. After talking for a while, he found out her first husband had passed away, and she was now a widower. Cathy never had any children, and she was all alone. She decided to move back to where her roots and family were, and to start living again. It was a shock for her to see Bill once again. They were both 47 years old, and eager to renew their friendship again.

Cathy loved the way Bill did everything. He would put his heart and soul into whatever he did. His motto was if you couldn't give it your best, don't do it at all. He was full of life and fun to be around. He was always the favorite uncle to all his nieces and nephews.

Bill sat down at the conference table among the different department heads. It was to be a short meeting, and then Bill would spend the afternoon uptown visiting some of his clients. At 1:05 the door opened and in walked the firms Vice

President, and Human Resources Manager. They were precise and to the point. They read from their power point presentation, the goals for the upcoming fourth quarter. When the meeting was over they pulled Bill aside to ask him a question.

"Bill, it recently was brought to my attention that you are an ex-chief in your local volunteer fire department."

"That's right Mr. Riley."

"Great, listen, I have to ask you a favor. John Robinson just resigned from the company and will be leaving in a few weeks. As you know he was the firm's Fire Safety Officer. According to our lease, we have to assign someone in our company this position." Bill nodded as he listened. "Well, I was hoping you would be our new Fire Safety Officer. All it entails is going to meetings with the building's management company twice a year, and making sure our office is evacuated during a fire drill, or God forbid, an actual emergency."

"Sure Mr. Riley, I'll do it. No problem at all."

"Great, that's one less thing for me to worry about. It's not like anything is going to happen, but if it did, I'm happy knowing you have experience in situations like this."

"I'll do my best."

"I know you will Bill, that's why I asked you. Brenda will get back to you with the date and time for the next safety meeting."

Thousands of people passed through the doorways of each city high rise on any given day. There was no way possible to account for everyone who entered and left each building. In case of a tragic event someone needed to know who was in the building. In the 1970's, many buildings asked their tenants to appoint a fire safety officer on each floor. This person would help in the evacuation process, and account for every employee in his or her firm. Most of the time, a senior employee, or a department head, filled the position. It was a job with a title, and no extra pay. Like everything he did in life, Bill would make sure he would do his best when it came to his newly appointed duties.

....

Alan Jenkins was busy filling out papers at the North Tower Information desk. In just over one month, he would be relaxing in a lounge chair on the deck of a luxurious cruise ship in the Caribbean. As the date got closer, he came to grips with his retirement decision. He no longer would have to get up at 4:00 in the morning and commute into Manhattan.

"Hi Alan, counting the days yet?"

"Not yet Annemarie, but almost."

"How are you doing today?"

"I'm doing great, but I can't believe how hard they make it for you to leave. Lots of paperwork to fill out."

"That's because no one wants you to leave Alan."

"Thanks Annemarie, how are the wedding plans coming?"

"Pretty good, I still can't find a dress I like. I think I've been to every store in Brooklyn and Manhattan."

"You'll find one, besides, you'll look beautiful in any dress you choose."

"Thanks Alan, and don't forget to give me your address before you leave. I'd love to have you and your wife come to the wedding."

"We both look forward to it, thanks...I won't forget."

Alan's compliment made Annemarie blush. She smiled, and returned to her office. She thought of Ralphie and hoped he was safe at work. She had to stop worrying about him so much, but it was hard to do. Her motherly instinct wanted to protect him.

As the summer was drawing to a close, people all over New York took advantage of the weather. On any given weekend, traffic would be backed up on the Long Island Expressway or Southern State Parkway as the parade of cars made their way to the Long Island beaches. People felt safe. They lived in a great country, and were born with freedom to choose their own destiny. They coped with the traffic and stalled cars for a few hours of peace and quiet on the sandy beaches.

Children were busy making sand castles, and swimmers were frolicking in the cold waves of the Atlantic Ocean. Women worked on their tans, and still others took the time to just relax, or people watch. What a diverse culture it was. There were light skinned people and dark skinned people, blondes and brunettes, and people who spoke different languages. This is what America was about. People coming together in diversity and learning how to respect and live with one another.

As everyone went about their lives, no one had a clue as to the events that were about to take place. If only they knew, they would have taken the time to make that one phone call. To call an old friend or family member, or to just tell someone they loved them. In one short month, New York would be a different place. Things were about to change, and normal would be a thing of the past.

CHAPTER 13

SEPTEMBER 11, 2001

On October 17, 1966, the fire alarm was sounded at 8:36pm for Box 55 598. The location was the Wonder Drug Store at 7 East 23rd Street in Manhattan. On this day, 12 New York City Firefighters would lose their lives in the line of duty.

Due to building renovations over the years, a five-inch concrete terrazzo floor had been installed on the ground level. The floor had concealed the raging inferno that was burning below the units inside of the building. When the floor collapsed, it took the lives of eight firefighters, two lieutenants, and two chiefs. This day would remain the most deadly day in FDNY history for 45 years. The events that were about to occur would not only change the FDNY, but a whole nation. September 11, 2001, would forever be etched in the minds of all Americans.

....

It was primary day in New York City. The polls would be open early so people could cast their ballots before going to work. It was an election year, and the people would be electing a new mayor in November. Rudy Giuliani had served two consecutive terms in office, and would be forced to pass the torch to a new mayor.

During his term, Giuliani helped to clean up the city, and crime was at an all time low. He helped to mend fences with the Fire and Police Unions, and would be remembered as one of the best mayors in New York City history. He cared about the city, its people, and its employees. Just a few weeks earlier he attended the funeral of another fallen firefighter. It was the fifth line of duty death this year. What made it worse was that he was a 27-year-old rookie firefighter. While battling a fire in Staten Island, he suffered a massive heart attack and died.

It was hard for everyone to cope with another death so soon after the Father's Day fire. The flags had been barely put back to full mast when Ralphie was told to lower the flag once again. He hoped it would be the last time in his career he had to do so, but knew that probably wouldn't be the case.

Once again history would repeat itself, but not in a way anyone would wish for. A young life was taken while answering the call to duty. When would this all stop? Five line of duty deaths in one year was five too many. Even though these brave men wore the best protective gear money could buy, it still wasn't enough.

....

6:00 am

Alan Jenkins was already busy at the information desk. A group of tourists were in the lobby waiting to ride the express elevator up to the Observation Deck. Alan had to tell them the tours did not begin until 9:00am. They had three more hours to wait, so he recommended they go eat breakfast at one of the coffee shops located on the lower level concourse. They reluctantly turned away, and would return later, as Alan directed them to do. After today, there would be only three more days until retirement. For the first time, Alan was excited with his decision. This last week at work would not be sad at all. No sir, it was going to be the best week ever.

Before leaving for work, Amy teased Alan about taking it easy. "Just do your job, and go out quietly. There's no need to get involved in anything that might hurt you."

"OK Amy, I understand. I won't go looking for trouble or chase away any bad guys," he said sarcastically.

"I'm serious Alan. I want to enjoy our vacation next week."

"Amy, what do you think is going to happen? Everything will be fine, OK."

"Yeah, I know, you're right. How are you feeling about all of this?"

"I'm happy with our decision. We should have done it sooner. I only wish we could have already been on the cruise like we originally planned. I'm really looking forward to it."

"Well, good things come to those who wait." Amy winked at Alan and the two embraced.

"I love you Amy."

"Me too Alan." He stared into her eyes longer than usual.

"What? Why are you staring at me like that?"

"Oh, nothing Amy. I just feel lucky to have you that's all. I promise to spend as much time with you as possible for now on." They kissed each other, and Alan headed off to work.

....

Six Probationary Firefighters reported to work this morning at various engine and ladder companies across the city. They were all fresh from the academy, and eager to start their new careers. Their lives, and their bright futures lay ahead of each of them. How exciting it was to finally be in real firehouses, and real life situations. They received the best training in the world, but now they faced the true test. They would be put in situations that were out of theirs, or anyone else's control. They would be real life situations with real people, and real victims. Sometimes new recruits would go weeks before seeing any real action. This would not be the case today. They would face a challenge never before experienced by anyone. An experience so horrible, thousands of lives would be affected in a matter of minutes.

....

Jimmy Valdez took the Number Two subway train to Wall Street. He was running a little late, but if there were no problems, he would be at work by 6:15am. A welder by trade, Jimmy had been a member of the Steelworkers Union for seven years. The money was good, but the job was not very rewarding. It was tedious, and he felt the only rewards went into the contractor's pockets.

Jimmy desired more in life. His brother Henry had recently become a New York City Police Officer, and encouraged him to take the test. It would be a cut in pay to start, but at least he would be helping people. Both jobs had their own dangers, but the life of a Police Officer became increasingly more appealing to him.

There were major building projects and remodeling jobs going on all over Manhattan. Jimmy had been working in the downtown area for quite some time now. It seemed like all the excitement took place uptown. Lower Manhattan was filled with your nine to five workers who put in a days work and went right home. As the train pulled into the Wall Street Station, Jimmy made up his mind. Next week he would walk down to 1 Police Plaza, and officially sign up to start the process of becoming a Police Officer.

....

"Hi honey, how are you today?"

"Oh, Annemarie, hi, I'm good, just waking up. Is everything OK?"

"Yes Ralphie, I just wanted to hear your voice before I went to work today. How is your shoulder feeling?"

"Oh, it's fine. Going down to headquarters this morning to the Department Doctor. Hopefully I'll be back on full duty tomorrow. What time is it anyway?"

"It is 6:15. I'm getting ready to hop in the shower. So, are we still on for tonight?"

"Of course. I'm looking forward to it. A nice quiet night with the lady I love. Am I picking up the movies, or are you?"

"I'll take care of it Ralphie. You go to the doctor and get better. I'll see you tonight."

"You got it. It's a date. I love you Annemarie."

"I love you too Ralphie."

Ralphie had an early morning appointment with the Department Doctor. While working at a basement fire a few weeks earlier, a metal cabinet fell over on him and injured his shoulder. He had been on medical leave ever since, and was chomping at the bit to return to the Palace. He missed seeing the guys, and missed playing with Ralphie Junior.

It had been a relatively quiet two weeks at the Palace. Every firefighter hopes that when they are on vacation or on leave, they don't miss the big one. No one likes to see damage to life or property, but if it had to happen, they wanted to be there to help.

Ralphie would drive down to the Department Medical Offices in Brooklyn, and then spend the rest of the day hanging out at the Palace. It would be good to hear everything that happened while he was gone. Around 6:00pm he would meet Annemarie for dinner.

....

Emily and Carl would rise each morning at 5:45am. They would then ride the train together all the way to the Trade Center. They enjoyed each other's company and found it made the ride to the city more bearable. Carl had been working long hours since his promotion. He got to the office early each day, and left later and later each night. Emily decided that she was just too tired to go in early today, and she would catch a later train to the city. The two would meet in the South Tower Lobby at 6:30, tonight and then ride back to Long Island together. As her pregnancy progressed, she found herself needing more and more rest.

Carl stood at the doorway watching his wife sleep. She looked so peaceful. Everything in life he cared about was right before his eyes. Every day that passed, brought them one day closer to having a family of their own. How precious life truly was. He loved to feel the baby move and kick. The life growing inside Emily truly was a gift from God.

Carl walked over to the bed and kissed Emily on her forehead. She smiled a smile of contentment. "Are you leaving already Carl?"

"Yeah, I have to plan for a staff meeting today. Don't worry though, I promise I'll be done by 6:15 so we can ride back from the city together."

"I'm going to hold you to that promise mister. You know, the only reason I married you was so I wouldn't have to ride the train by myself anymore." Emily giggled and pulled Carl closer so she could give him a kiss. "I'll be waiting for you in the Lobby. Don't be late."

"O.K. Emily, thanks, I'll see you tonight. Call me when you get to your office. I love you."

"I will, bye Carl, I love you too."

....

"Hi Jane, did I wake you?"

"No, I've been up for a while Richie. You know I don't sleep well when you're not home. How was work last night?"

"Slow, nothing past midnight though. We had a car fire right before dinner."

"Good, you'll be able to mow the lawn when you get back then."

Jane smiled as she said those words to Richie. There were times when Richie would work the night tour and come home with no sleep at all. After an all night fire, he would catch the early morning sun rising over the rooftops of the neighborhood brownstones.

"I should be home at about 9:30."

"That's fine Richie. I'll leave here by 8:15. I should be home by 4:00. I'm glad you're not working again tonight. We always miss you when you work a twenty-four. Seems like you are gone forever."

"Well, I don't have to be back at work until Thursday, so you'll be seeing a lot of me the next few days."

"Did you watch the Giants game last night Richie? What happened to our Super Bowl team from January?" Jane was an avid football fan. Before meeting Richie she hated to watch any sport. Over the years she learned how to love the games, the strategies, and the athleticism that went into each of them.

"Yeah, unfortunately I did. I fell asleep in the fourth quarter. I guess I didn't miss much though."

"No you didn't. I turned the game off at halftime."

"How are the kids?"

"Wonderful. They left early for school. They seem to be enjoying the new school year."

"Good. I'm looking forward to seeing all of you later."

"O.K. Richie. If I don't get in the shower soon, I'm going to be late. I love you honey. See you tonight."

"I love you too Jane. Bye."

They both hung up the phone and began their day. Neither of them knew how it would all play out.

As Richie looked out the second story window of the Palace, he saw the beginning of a beautiful September morning. According to the news on the radio, it would be an unseasonably warm bright day. Just when you thought summer was over, a day like today would come around just to tease you.

Richie was in no hurry to rush home today. His tour wouldn't officially end for another few hours. In the meantime, the Palace was beginning to come to life. Some of the guys were packing their laundry to take home, while their replacements were beginning their commutes from the suburbs, and various parts of the city. It was Richie's favorite time of the day. The Palace kitchen would become crowded with everyone sitting around drinking coffee, and talking about their families, or the score of last night's game.

Something was different this morning. It was an indescribable feeling Richie had. He felt anxious, but didn't know why. Ever since Rebecca's death this feeling would just pop up. He hadn't thought about Rebecca for months, but she was on his mind today. The last thing Richie, wanted was to be alone today. He would stay at the firehouse a little longer than usual. Hopefully, the feeling, and the images of Rebecca would go away.

....

The boarding process was underway at Boston's Logan Airport. It was a relatively quiet day. Most of the people needing to fly on business would leave on Monday. Tuesday flights tended to be more relaxed, and the boarding process proceeded without a hitch. With blue skies predicted all across the country, it would be a beautiful day to fly. Visibility was high, and there was not much turbulence.

United Airlines Flight 175 took off at 7:58am with 56 passengers aboard. One minute later American Airlines Flight 11 followed. The two planes were headed on a nonstop course for Los Angeles International Airport. Not much is known what happened during the next twenty minutes, but the deadly plot that had been planned months before, was underway.

....

The big clock in Penn Station read 8:10 am. With any luck at all Emily should be at her desk by 8:30. She waited on the subway platform for the #1 IRT train to take her downtown to the World Trade Center. After a ten-minute wait, an announcement came over the public address system. A train was stuck on the downtown tracks. This caused all the other trains traveling in the same direction to be delayed. There would be no service to downtown until the train could be removed from the tracks. At 8:25am service resumed, and Emily boarded the train. Little did she know how this delay would affect the rest of her life?

Emily entered the North Tower lobby and said hello to Alan Jenkins, as she passed by the information desk. The lobby was filled with people coming and going in all different directions. She walked past the line of tourists waiting to go up to the observation deck, and to the bank of elevators that would take her to her office. She pressed the button and waited for the elevator to arrive. The subway delay caused her to be late, but it was out of her control. She would be staying until 6:15 tonight, so she did not feel so guilty about being late for work. It seemed like everything was moving in slow motion today. As she waited, she felt a sudden violent rumble rip through the tower. A few seconds later, as she looked out the large glass windows she could see debris falling. Her first instinct was to run, but it was already too late. Just as Emily was about to turn away the elevator doors opened and a large ball of bright orange flames jumped out and engulfed her. It was 8:46am and American Airlines flight #11 from Boston had just crashed into the North Tower.

Emily's hair and clothes burned from her body. She heard the cries of onlookers who ran to her aid. The voices and screaming seemed to become faint, and she immediately started to lose consciousness. The pain was excruciating, and all she could think about at this very moment was her husband and her baby. She did not know what happened, but she vowed to herself to fight through the pain. She did not come this far in her pregnancy, for it to all go away. She was determined to live, and to hold her baby, and her husband in her arms.

Alan Jenkins was the first to arrive to Emily's aid. He grabbed a portable fire extinguisher that he kept under the Information Desk. He pulled the safety pin, and began to spray Emily with the cold water. The elevator shaft was now an inferno, as burning aviation fuel spilled down the shaft to the floors below. It ignited everything in its path. People were running through the lobby to the nearest exits. Alan did not know if the woman he was trying to help was dead or alive. He did not even recognize her, even though he saw her only seconds before. As he grabbed her by the wrists to pull her away from the smoke and fire, he felt her skin pull away from its bone. He knew right away this would be no ordinary day. He would do whatever it took to get this woman, and everyone else to safety.

....

At 8:47am the first of 18 fire companies began responding to a fifth alarm fire at box 8087 on the corner of West Street and Vecsey Street. Before arriving at the scene, a second fifth alarm was transmitted by the first arriving Battalion Chief. He immediately set up a command post in the lobby of the North Tower.

Alan Jenkins carried Emily's badly burned body to the first ambulance he saw. Although her condition seemed grave, the paramedics found a faint pulse and rushed her off to St. Vincent's Hospital. She slipped in and out of consciousness during the short ride to the hospital. She could hear the voices of everyone around her, but could not answer them. She heard only voices, but saw no faces. She wanted to scream "help me, please don't let me or my baby die," but her throat was also burned by the smoke and superheated gases she breathed in. Once again, she thought of Carl. She had to tell him where she was. He would be expecting her to call when she arrived at the office.

Back at the North Tower, Alan was busy directing the arriving units to the interior stairwells that were not damaged in the crash. He still did not know that a plane had crashed into the building. He felt the rumble and saw the flames, but in his mind, thought this was 1993 all over again. He first found out about the crash when he overheard some of the fleeing people tell the firefighters about the plane that had flown directly into the tower.

He knew right away this was not some random accident.

....

Richie had just changed out of his uniform when he heard the screaming coming from the day room. Everyone was huddled around the television set. He rushed down the stairs just in time to see the flames shooting from the huge hole in the side of the tower. Captain Farley was shouting orders for everyone to get ready. Since the tour change had just occurred, many of the men going off duty were still present. He knew no one wanted to be left behind, and compiled a list of who was responding to the call. If there was one thing that was needed on a call like this, it was manpower.

They all stared at the television knowing people were trapped on the upper floors. Whatever faith the firefighters had, it was time to ask God for help. A silence fell over the Palace as the men waited to hear the call go out for their companies to respond. Since they were located just across the river, they figured they would be one of the first units called. They loaded extra air tanks and tools onboard the rigs in preparation of the battle they were all willing to take part in. Each man knew that this was the biggest challenge they would face in their career as a firefighter.

Richie called home on his cell phone. He knew no one was there, but he called anyway. "Jane, kids, hi, it's me. I'm not sure if you know what is happening but you will soon enough. We're getting ready to get called in and I just wanted to tell all of you not to wait for me for dinner. This is big. I'll probably be home late. Don't worry about me. I'll be okay. I promise to cut the lawn tomorrow, Jane. I love you guys." He hung up the phone just as the tones at the Palace began to ring. Within a minute, the rigs were on their way. They raced to the scene with their red lights flashing, and sirens and air horns blasting loudly.

From the rigs they could see the smoke from across the river fill the light blue sky. They raced down Court Street to Cadman Plaza, and to the entrance of the Brooklyn Bridge. Ladder 179 was right behind Engine 200. As they crossed the bridge, the enormity of the situation became reality. This was not a scene on television anymore, but life in its worst degree. They saw the gaping hole in the steel and glass structure. Whatever they thought, there would be no turning back. The closer they got, each of them sensed that this trip might be a one-way ticket. No one had ever seen a fire this large. It would take a long time to climb each step one at a time just to reach the fire. Whatever it took, they would try to get the job done.

Ladder 179 and Engine 200 parked on West Street. The drivers stayed with the rigs, while the officers and men proceeded to the command post in the lobby. Bobby Giordano spotted one of the department's Chaplains. "Hey Padre, make sure you say a prayer for me too will you. I need all the help I can get." The Chaplain nodded and continued to pray. As they approached the building, the horror of the day took on a whole new meaning. Millions of pieces of paper filled the sky. It was flying out of the hole in the building, far above them, and landing in the streets. It was all over the place. The paper seemed to float lazily to the ground. In the middle of all the papers, there were other objects falling faster and faster. They seemed to pick up speed as they got closer to the ground. They hit with a loud thud and exploded on impact. Louie Ludwig wept openly as he saw the falling objects were people. They were choosing to jump to their own deaths instead of perishing in a blazing inferno.

Everyone was shaken up by what they just saw, but they continued on into the Tower. They broke up into small groups and reported to the command post. They then started the slow climb up the stairwells. "I'm glad the kid isn't here today Richie."

"Yeah, me too Louie. This is bad. I don't feel good about this one."

"Me too, I know what you mean."

"Hang in there Louie, we'll be o.k, just pray. It will make you feel better."

"I've never been much of a praying man until now, but I want to see my wife and kids tonight."

....

Bill Vogler was at his desk and saw the plane hit the North Tower. It reminded him of all those disaster movies he had seen over the years. It was so beyond belief; that he had to remind himself what he just saw was real. There was panic throughout the whole office as people screamed and ran for the elevators and stairs. An announcement was made not to panic, and to evacuate the building in a safe manner.

In Bill's mind, some poor pilot just lost his life and the lives of everyone on his plane by drifting off course and crashing into the tower. This had to be the reason for the accident, because everyone knew airplanes didn't fly over lower Manhattan. What a pity. At this point no one knew that this was not an accident, but a deliberate act of terrorism.

As the people fled to the exits, Bill volunteered to stay behind for a while to answer the phones. He knew there would be many worried relatives calling to make sure their loved ones were okay. At 9:02am he hung up the phone just as his cell phone began to ring. "Bill, thank God it's you. I just saw the accident on the news, what happened down there? Where are you? Are you okay? Cathy was in panic. Her words were choppy, and she was talking very fast.

"I'm in my office answering the phones, I'm okay. We're evacuating the building, but I'm safe here Cathy."

"Billy, I'd feel better if you left too. Don't be some hero, besides, everyone else is leaving. Get out of there now."

"I know, I know, don't worry. I'll stay for a few more minutes and then head down. I want to make sure the floor is clear first. They didn't make me the Safety Officer for nothing." Cathy's eyes were glued to the television screen as she watched the tower burn. As she watched the picture before her, she thought she saw another plane heading towards the towers. At first she thought it must be a replay of original accident. After a few seconds she realized her mistake and began to yell. "Billy, get out now," she screamed, "there's another plane, and it's headed your way. No, oh no, Billy." As she fell to her knees weeping, the phone suddenly went dead, as she watched the moment of impact.

....

Ralphie reported to FDNY headquarters in Brooklyn at 8:15am. He was hoping to be cleared to full active duty today. The last few weeks of rest and relaxation were okay, but now it was time to get back to the job he loved.

After signing in, he was forced to wait, as the doctor was behind schedule. At about 9:00am he heard the news about what was happening across the river in Manhattan. His first thoughts were immediately of Annemarie. Which building was hit? What floors were hit? He needed the details, and he needed them right away. Now was not the time to panic. He would try to stay calm, but he was suddenly overcome with fear. He called Annemarie's office, but there was no answer. He tried her cell phone, but the call did not go through. After a few minutes, he tried again, and the line was busy. He thought that was a good sign.

A few minutes later, all appointments with the doctor were cancelled. Even though he was officially still on medical leave, Ralphie knew where he needed to be. He needed to be down at the Trade Center with his brothers from Engine 200. He would do anything it took to find Annemarie and get her to safety. He ran to his car and started to drive into Manhattan. He reached the Brooklyn Bridge just when the Mayor had ordered all bridges and tunnels into the city closed. He begged with the officer to let him by. After seeing his department badge, and how frantic he looked, the officer let him by. Ralphie's car would be the last one to cross the bridge into Manhattan this morning.

People were fleeing Manhattan as fast as they could. The Brooklyn Bridge was filled with cars, trucks, and pedestrians all exiting the city. Lower Manhattan was under attack. He called Annemarie five more times but still could not get through to her. "God, please help me. Help Annemarie. Help everyone we need you. We need you bad," Ralphie prayed out loud. He heard the reports on the radio about people jumping from the buildings. "Please God, don't let Annemarie be one of them."

....

Anthony and Lucille Margulo were getting ready to go shopping when they heard the news. They knew Annemarie worked on the 94th floor of the North Tower. From the images they saw on the television, it looked like the crash was below that floor. Immediately Lucille began to cry hysterically as she thought about her only daughter. She picked up the phone and tried to call Annemarie. There was no answer. She then tried Annemarie's cell phone, and after a few rings Annemarie answered. "Annemarie, oh my God, are you alright?"

"Mama, oh mama, it's awful. We're trapped. We can't get down. The fire is getting hotter and, and" she paused, "people are jumping." She broke down and cried. It was comforting to hear her mother's voice, but she still was very scared.

"Annemarie," Anthony shouted into the phone, "Annemarie, are you hurt?"

"No daddy, I'm o.k. There are a lot of people hurt real bad. It's terrible. I don't know what to do." She was in shock. The impact caused her to hit her head against her desk. "Help me daddy, someone help us please."

"Hang in there honey. The whole Fire Department is responding. Go to the roof if it gets too hot. They'll figure out a way. I know those guys. They'll get you out."

"Daddy, please, go get Joey from school and tell him I'm o.k."

"I will. Don't hang up, keep talking to me."

"O.k., I love you Daddy. I won't hang...." The phone went dead and Anthony dialed frantically to get her back. Lucille sat there and cried. Her baby was trapped. She longed to see her, and to hold her. She had to try to stay positive, but the pictures on the television were frightening. At least she knew Annemarie was still alive.

....

Carl Risland felt the building shake on impact. A few seconds later, he saw the horror of people falling to their deaths. The South Tower had been hit and he had to get out. He ran to one stairwell and the door was jammed and would not open. He ran to the one across the hall, and it was still intact. Smoke billowed down the stairwell like a giant chimney in reverse. The plane had hit the building at about the 78th floor. In a matter of seconds, people were filling the stairwells. They had all been working at their desks when the second plane hit. An intense fire immediately grew, and it took out everything in its path. People were sucked out the windows from the force of the impact and fell to their deaths. The fire quickly spread out of control to the to the floors immediately above and below the impact zone.

All Carl could think about was his wife Emily, and the baby. She should have already been to work at the time the first plane hit. If she were at her desk, would she be okay? He hoped Emily had slept in later than usual this morning. "Oh please God, this can't be happening. Do something, please, help us all."

The stairwells were filled with people all walking in the same direction. They were all frightened and fighting for their lives. Each step they took got them closer to safety. All of a sudden, everyone came to a standstill. No one was running, they could hardly move. Hundreds of people from each floor below were also trying to flee. The only sounds you heard were the sound of people's feet hitting each step. No one spoke. They just waited to get down and out of the building as quickly as possible.

....

It was now 9:20am, and three companies of firefighters reached the 40th floor of the South Tower. They were in constant contact with the command post located in the lobby. Over in the North Tower, it was a completely different story. The radio messages being sent to the firefighters climbing the stairwells were not being heard.

As Richie and the crews of 179 and 200 climbed each step, all they thought about was the job that lay ahead of them when they reached the impact zone. How many victims were there? Would anyone still be alive? They raced up those stairs with every intention of putting out the fire, and saving as many lives as possible.

By this time, a borough call had been sent out calling all available units. The department's resources would be stretched thin all over the city. With each step the firefighters took, their adrenaline flowed more and more. Each of them wore forty pounds of equipment, and carried with them extra hose, air bottles, and tools. By the time they reached the fire, would they have any strength left to do their jobs?

Louie Ludwig had a feeling that this was it, the final fire, his last call. In spite of this feeling he kept on going. If his brothers were there, so was he. He saw fear on the face of every person who passed him going in the opposite direction on the stairwell. Some of them were burned, and others were bleeding. He could have taken the easy way out and escorted them down the stairs, but if he did, how would he be able to live with himself? They were all scared. Each and every firefighter who climbed those stairs was scared. Every one of them was a father, a brother, a husband or an uncle. Someone loved each of them. They worked through their fear, and kept on going.

....

Ralphie crossed over the Brooklyn Bridge and traffic came to a complete standstill. The streets were filled with thousands of people all moving in the same direction. They were fleeing Manhattan. Some of them had even hopped onto the backs of trucks and trailers. In the true spirit of compassion, some were carrying others who needed help, or were too scared to continue. When people are in need, there will always be someone to rise to the occasion and show compassion.

It was impossible for Ralphie to drive any further. He jumped out of his car and started running. His cell phone began to ring, and he stopped to answer it. He recognized the number, and his heart began to race. Tears began to fall from his eyes when he heard Annemarie's voice. She was frightened and sought comfort in Ralphie. "Annemarie, where are you, are you out of the building?"

"Oh Ralphie, we're trapped. There is no where to go." She was now crying uncontrollably. "I don't know what to do. I'm so scared."

"O.k., calm down, take a deep breath, where are you now?"

"We couldn't stay in our office anymore. The fire and heat was too much. It was terrible Ralphie. People are jumping. The building is making noises too....and the walls, the walls are all starting to crack."

"Hang in there, Annemarie. I just crossed the bridge. I'm running towards the building now." As he said this he looked up and saw both towers burning out of control. He knew Annemarie was in there, but he felt helpless. He would do anything he could to get to her.

"I'm losing hope Ralphie, I'm scared."

"Don't ever lose hope Annemarie, pray. God will be there for you." After he said that he began to pray together with Annemarie. "Father God, please comfort the people who are in the building. Send them an angel to comfort them, and hold them by the hand. Give me, and all the firefighters, all the strength you can, to help these people. Please bring your peace, and your love, to this overwhelming situation. We love you father, help us now, in our time of need."

"Oh Ralphie, I love you so much. I don't think I'm going to make it out of here." Her voice trembled as she spoke.

"Don't say that. You'll be o.k."

"Promise me you'll be there for Joey. Help him get through this. He loves you Ralphie. If I don't come home, please be a part of his life. He can't lose both of us."

Ralphie fought back the tears when he heard those words. Of course he would be there for Joey, but he wanted to be there for Annemarie also. He wanted to be a family.

"Tell Joey, and mom and dad that I love them."

"You'll tell them later when you get home. Don't talk like that."

"Ralphie, I'm o.k. Don't worry about me anymore. I'm starting to accept this, it's all right. I'm sorry I'm leaving you like this. You made me enjoy life again. I'll never forget you Ralphie. I love you."

"Oh Annemarie, I love you too." The tears poured down Ralphie's face as he could no longer bottle up his emotions. "Don't lose hope."

"We're going up to the roof Ralphie, we have to get out of here now." The phone suddenly went silent. Ralphie tried to call back but could not get through. All over the city, thousands of calls were being made from frantic relatives to family members. The system couldn't handle the number of calls being made anymore. Ralphie ran towards the towering infernos, all the time thinking only of Annemarie.

....

At 9:32 am the command post in the North Tower was frantically calling all units in the building back down to the lobby. It became very clear that the buildings were now unsafe. The department had to regroup and come up with another course of action. Some of the radios heard the orders, but others didn't. Some heard the order, but out of loyalty to their profession, or thoughts of the trapped people, ignored it. They were willing to do whatever it took to save a life. Once again, the issue of the radios would come into play. Richie, Lt. Farley, and Louie Ludwig had now reached the 32nd floor. None of them heard the message. The other firefighters from the Palace were scattered throughout the building. The guys from Engine 200 were busy helping a group of victims on the twentieth floor. The only way to help these people was to drop their tools and extra hose, and help them down to safety. Captain Shields made the decision that would save their lives.

Bobby Giordano and Vinny Amarosa could go on no further. They reached the 30th floor and collapsed. Vinny was out of breath, and was having trouble breathing. Bobby was busy trying to raise Lt. Farley on the radio. He knew Vinny was in trouble and couldn't just leave him to fend for himself. He took an oath to never leave a brother behind. The situation on the stairwells grew more intense as thousands of people filed down one by one. "Vinny, come on, get up and give me your arm. I'm getting you out of here."

"No Bobby, leave me here in one of the offices. You go on. I'll be fine. I'll catch up to you later."

"You know I can't do that Vinny. We came in here together, and we'll leave together too."

"I don't know if I can even make it down the stairs, besides, they need your help up there more than I do."

"I'm not leaving you Vinny. Get that thought out of your head. I'm taking you out of here even if I have to carry you down myself. Now, get up." Vinny put his arm around Bobby's shoulder and pulled himself up. They walked out of the stairwell and into an office. It was an eerie feeling. As they looked around they saw desks, but no people. Everyone left in a hurry. There were coffee mugs on the desks, and steam was still rising out of them. By now, Vinny's chest had tightened, and his breathing became labored. He looked over to the wall and motioned over to Bobby. "Bobby, look, the walls are cracking. That's not a good sign. This whole thing is going to go down."

"Let's go Vinny, we got to get out of here." The two men started the slow climb down the mountain of stairs. They felt bad that they were heading down, while others were still going up.

"Bobby, if I don't make it out of here, tell my family that I love them, will you."

"You got it Vinny. Hang in there."

Richie, Louie, and Lt. Farley had now reached the 38th floor. The higher up they got, the building became louder, like it was crying out in pain from the injuries it had sustained. There were creaks, loud bangs, and the sound of wind blowing into the building from its wounds. Although the three men knew they were in danger, they kept on moving.

....

The scene was the same in the South Tower. Many of the people started down to safety when the North Tower was hit. A few minutes later they were told to return to their offices. Some of them did, but others continued on to safety. Debris was flying down onto the Plaza outside the two buildings, and someone in command thought it would be safer if everyone stayed inside.

Carl Risland kept heading down with the others. All he wanted was to get to safety and find Emily. When this was all over, they would look back on this day and thank God for sparing their lives. He decided to tell Emily not to wait until October to leave her job, but to leave it now. Her life, and the baby's life, were more important to him. It was now 9:45 am and a group of firefighters had just reached the impact zone on the 78th floor of the South Tower. What they saw was gruesome. It was a scene right out of hell. Death surrounded them. There were no survivors here. They now knew there was nothing they could do for the poor souls above them. The fire was burning out of control, and without a miracle, their fates were bleak.

When the planes hit, they were both loaded with fuel for their cross-country flights. The fuel was now spilled through out both buildings. It found every opening, every hole, and every nook and cranny. As it seeped through, it spread its deadly venom and breathed its deadly fire.

Steel beams begin to melt when exposed to temperatures of 1000 degrees Fahrenheit for extended periods of time. Jet fuel burns at 1200 degrees Fahrenheit. As the fuel burned freely, it consumed everything in its path. With every new fire, the flames grew even hotter. Slowly, the burning steel began to melt. The impact of the crash had knocked most of the fireproofing off of the exposed beams and joists. They began to soften to the point of bending. As they bent, the pressure from the floors above became greater and greater.

Richard Damante

Dozens of firefighters were waiting at the South Tower command post for orders. As more units responded, radio communications became more chaotic. There was even a report of a third plane heading straight for Manhattan. It was time to give up the fight. The rescue mission would have to be abandoned. As the radio message went out, the lives of thousands were left in the hands of God.

Carl Risland was now on the 21st floor landing. He was out of breath, but wouldn't stop. He made eye contact with the firefighters as they passed him going in the opposite direction. He saw the fear in their eyes, but they still continued on. With every step he took, that look of fear was etched in his mind. One of the firefighters looked so young. He had an orange probationary shield on his helmet. "Poor kid," Carl thought to himself. He looked at the kid again and held out his hand. He placed it on the shoulder of the young firefighter just long enough to say the words "God be with you." This brave young man just nodded, and continued on. What would make a man go on in a situation like this? Carl knew it couldn't be the money. These men were just like him. Some older, some younger, but they were men. Mere mortals. They felt the same fear as Carl, and they stared it right in the eye.

Slowly, the South Tower began to shake. It began to breathe its last breath. It screamed out loud as the top floors began to drop one by one on top of each other. The floors below them could not withstand the extra weight, and in what looked like slow motion, the building began to turn to powder.

Carl heard a large rumble. With every step he took, the noise got louder and louder. Panic and screams filled the stairwell. People cried out to God, and for their families. Alan knew that his life was about to end. He had looked forward to starting his own family, but now he would not be a part of their lives. The last words he whispered were "I love you Emily. Give the baby a kiss for me. I'll see you both in heaven some day." He felt no pain, and felt the hand of God on his shoulder.

....

Joey Donovan and Willy Johnson watched in horror as the South Tower collapsed. Not in their wildest imaginations, could they see something like this happening. Sure, maybe part of the building might collapse, but not the whole building. They had been ordered upon arrival to stay with their rigs. They wanted to help, but an order was an order. They no longer could bear to just stand by and watch the death and destruction. Their brothers were in those two towers and needed their help. It hit them hard. How many men were already lost in the South Tower collapse? They didn't have time to cry, as a tidal wave of smoke and debris filled the streets of downtown Manhattan.

....

Over in the North Tower, Alan Jenkins had left the information desk and headed up the stairs a few minutes earlier. He remembered Amy's words about not getting hurt. He could have run the other way, or just ran out like the others, but how could he live with himself if he did that. By now, the buildings power was all but gone. He could not stand to hear the noise of the numerous people jumping to their deaths. He had to do something. He spent the last 40 years of his life helping people, and today would not be an exception. Over his radio he heard that there was a group of people on the 19th floor waiting for help. They could not make it down the stairs by themselves. They had suffered either burns or broken bones during the initial impact. There were others who were just too old to make the climb down 19 flights of stairs. He spotted Joey Donovan and Willy Johnson and asked for their help. He escorted them up a rear stairwell. When they got there, Willy and Joey immediately started to carry the injured down to safety.

"Alan, Alan, don't leave me here." Alan turned and saw Sylvia Harris sitting in a chair crying. Sylvia had worked in the buildings ever since they were built. She was scared and unable to continue any further on her own. "Don't worry Sylvia, we're gonna get out of here." He picked her up and began to carry her down one step at a time. His arms ached, but a promise was a promise. As they slowly descended, others rushed by them, or pushed them out of their way. It didn't matter to Alan though; he would get Sylvia to safety no matter how long it took him. Neither Alan nor the others in the stairwells knew the South tower had collapsed.

....

Annemarie was losing hope of getting out alive. From their vantage point, they witnessed the South Tower collapse. They all knew, that if help didn't arrive soon, they would meet the same fate. When faced with this decision some chose their own way to die. Annemarie watched as a man and a woman embraced each other, held hands, and then jumped.

As long as Annemarie had breath she had life. She had Joey and Ralphie to think about too.

When faced with this situation, most turned to prayer. They had to face the situation and put their faith in God. Some asked for more time on earth, while others asked for forgiveness. If they survived, they promised to make changes in their lives. As they prayed, peace began to fall upon them. Their lives were now in God's hands. Every one of their prayers was heard. Their prayers for salvation would not be ignored.

Annemarie dialed her home phone one last time. As the phone rang, she thought about what to say. How should she say good- bye? The answering machine came on and she heard Joey's voice. "Hi, you have reached the home of Annemarie and Joey. We are not home right now so please leave a message." The answering machine then beeped, and Annemarie began to speak. "Hi Joey, it's me mom." She tried to stay strong for Joey, and not cry. "I just wanted to tell you not to worry about me. I don't know if I'll be home tonight. I want you to be a big boy and listen to grandma and grandpa, okay. I want you to know that I love you very much Joey, and I always will. You were a gift from God, and now I'm in God's hands Joey. I don't know why this is happening, but Joey, honey, please, keep your faith in God. Be strong, and be brave. Don't cry. I'll be okay. Ralphie loves you too Joey. He'll be there for you also. Bye baby, mommy loves you."

She tried to dial Ralphie one more time, but couldn't stand to say goodbye to him. She wished he would continue on without her, and sat back and waited for the end to come. Perfect strangers became best friends in the final minutes of their lives. They would not die alone. They were there to comfort each other until the very end. One life would touch another, no life without a meaning. They each had families of their own, but now, they would become a new family. Evil would win this battle, but love would win the day.

....

Like the South Tower, the North Tower's death would come from within. Just like a twin that lost a sibling, the North Tower could not stand without the other. As she watched her twin die, she felt its pain. As the minutes went by, the pain inside her grew. She would stand as long as possible to make sure more and more people got to safety. When the pain, and the weight became too much for her, she would breathe one last breath. She had served the city well, and in a matter of minutes, she would be no more.

Maydays were being transmitted throughout the building. If only the messages got through, the loss of life might not have been as great. The new digital radios caused a delay in the transmissions. Because of the buildings size and construction, many of the signals were lost.

A large group of firefighters were spread out through the entire building. They were standing by for orders, when the order to evacuate was sent. The ones that heard it were angry; knowing that the job they came to do was not done. They had tried, but they failed. Richie, Lt. Farley, and Louie still did not hear the message to evacuate. They had met up on a higher floor with a group of firefighters from one of the Rescue companies.

The situation looked grim. To a man, they knew this was to be their final call to duty. There would be no more fires to fight, no more firehouse chatter, and no more families to tell them how much they were loved. Death was quickly circling all around them. The air turned thick, and it began to suffocate them. The interior walls were cracking, and some began to fall. The men were all exhausted, and their bodies overheating. Some had taken off their protective coats and sat down to cry or to pray. They didn't have the strength to go one step further. This scene was being repeated throughout the building. They hoped that when the time came, it would be quick and painless. When they prayed, their final prayers were for the families they would leave behind.

As the tears mixed with the sweat falling down Richie's face, he stood up and began to speak. "Lord, I ask you for forgiveness upon my soul, and the souls of everyone of your children here today." Each man, no matter what his religious convictions were, bowed his head and prayed with Richie. They thanked God for everything he gave them, and for the chance to be a New York City firefighter. If their time had now come, they accepted their fate, and waited. Lt. Farley started to recite the Lord's Prayer. One by one they each joined in. "....and lead us not, into temptation, but deliver us from evil." As the saying goes, there are no atheists in foxholes. The same thing happened in those stairwells. They called on Jesus to save them. They would be saved, but in a much different way.

I'm sorry Richie, sorry Louie."

"For what L.T.?"

"For this, for bringing you into this mess. I've led a full life. I'm 61 years old."

"Hey Lieutenant, don't be sorry, this isn't over yet, besides, I have a feeling, this is only the beginning."

"Thanks Richie."

Richie and Louie both saluted the Lieutenant as the building began to shake. As each floor above them came falling down, the sound became louder and louder. The three men held each other's hands, and crawled up in a ball. They called on the name of Jesus over and over again. Like an approaching freight train bearing down on them, the floors began to let loose. The light of day turned into darkness of night. Everyone left in the building that called on the name of God was not alone. Angels swarmed down and held each of their hands. Their fears all went away. One by one the floors tumbled down, and death came quick. Through it all, they felt no pain.

In a matter of seconds, it was over. The darkness of night burst into the brightest daylight any of them had ever seen. Silence filled the air, and a beautiful calming wind swept over them. The clouds opened up and the voices of heaven were heard in the distance. There was no more sadness. No evil. Instead, there was only peace, laughter, and joy. Their prayers had been answered, as Jesus took each of their hands, and lead them through the gates of heaven.

People always say there is no crying in heaven, but on this day, that was not true. As Richie and the others entered the kingdom, they all fell down on their knees and cried. They cried tears of joy, as their rewards were bestowed upon them. They saw friends, familiar faces, and loved ones. They saw little Rebecca smiling. She was right there holding Jesus' hand. Thousands entered the kingdom that day. In heaven they were all the same. No heroes. No titles, just children of God.

....

As the building pancaked down upon itself, the streets were covered in ash and rubble. A great white cloud ominously moved down the streets engulfing everything in its path. The white powdery substance covered everyone. Cars and trucks were buried or crushed. Then, as fast as it all happened, there was silence. The only sound heard was the chirping of the pass alarms on the bodies of the fallen firefighters.

Buried somewhere within the pile of jagged steel were the bodies of Richie, Lieutenant Farley, and Louie Ludwig. Annemarie, Carl Risland, Bill Vogler, and Alan Jenkins were also somewhere in the ominous pile of death and debris. Their lives were all cut short due to the hatred someone had for their fellow man. Their families would never get another chance to say I love you.

Those who survived picked themselves up and wondered if they were dead or alive. They were all in a state of shock, but thankful to be alive. Their emotions changed with each passing second. Happiness turned to sadness as the big picture began to sink in. In the hours that followed there was hope. The FDNY recalled every firefighter to report to duty. Stretch Dolan got to the scene minutes after the first tower collapsed. He pulled on his gear and grabbed a group of firefighters that got separated from their companies. One by one they mounted the pile of debris. They immediately began to dig with their hands. If anyone was still alive in there, they were determined to find him or her.

As minutes turned to hours, the scene became grimmer. Instead of finding survivors, all they were finding were remnants of human life. Everything they found they treated with dignity. Both buildings were 110 stories tall. They were filled with hundreds of offices. Each office had desks, tables, chairs, telephones, and computers. There were none of these in the pile. As the men searched, they heard cell phones ringing below them, somewhere in the pile. In an effort to locate their loved ones, family members were calling cell phones, hoping the rescuers would hear them. It was frustrating to hear the ringing, and not be able to find the person it belonged to.

Initial reports were that 10,000 people were feared dead, and many more injured. Because the attack took place the same time the daily day tour began, many companies responded with extra men from the night tour. It would be days before an accurate number of the missing firefighters could be verified. They all knew the number would be high, but no one could imagine just how high the number would climb.

After hours of digging through the pile, Captain Dolan's radio suddenly came to life. Someone kept keying his microphone. This caused static and a high-pitched yelp, but no voice was heard. After a few minutes of this, Stretch thought he heard a very faint voice. "This is Captain Dolan, Ladder 179. We hear your calls. Who are you?" After getting up enough strength to talk, a voice was heard from deep within the pile. "Somebody help me. I'm trapped. I can't move."

"O.K., keep talking to me. What's your name? What is your location?"

"This is Lieutenant Barnes. I'm in the downstairs shopping mall under the South Tower. What happened?" After thinking for a few seconds, Captain Dolan answered. He chose his words carefully in order to give the man hope. He probably did not know that both towers had come down. There was no need to alarm the poor guy even more. Even though they now knew his location, how would they find him in all this mess? There were 220 stories of building on top of him. "You hang in there Lieutenant. The building collapsed. Is there anyone there with you?"

"Yes, two of my men, but they didn't make it."

"What injuries do you have L.T.? Can you move at all?"

"I think my legs are both broken, and I'm pinned under some heavy steel beams. I can barely move my arms, and the pain is getting worse. You gotta get me out of here Captain."

Knowing there was someone alive gave the rescuers hope. They knew there had to be others too. The enemy now became time. How long could Lieutenant Barnes survive in his situation? How long could anyone else survive? After a few more hours, the hope was beginning to turn to despair. They hadn't even made a dent in the pile, and still no survivors. As day turned into night, Lieutenant Barnes had lost all his hope of being rescued. He asked for the Department Chaplain to pray with him. After Stretch broke the news to him that the Chaplain did not survive, Lieutenant Barnes began to weep. "Hey, Captain Dolan, look at that. The Chaplain must be up in heaven already, waiting for me to join him."

"We're going to get you, hang in there." Stretch knew his words were there to provide comfort for the trapped man. It would take a miracle to find him and bring him out alive, but no one was ready to give up the fight.

"I can't hold out much longer Captain. Can you do me a favor?"

"Sure, just name it, what can I do for you?"

"Can you give my wife and kids a message for me."

There was now a crowd surrounding Captain Dolan. They were listening to the messages of their trapped brother.

"Okay, what do you need L.T.?"

"You tell them that I held on as long as I could, that I didn't give up. Tell my wife I'm sorry for everything I ever did to hurt her." With each passing minute his words got weaker as he gasped for air. "Tell my kids I'm proud of them, and to take good care of their mother for me. Make sure you do this for me, and tell all of them, that I love them. They were all I thought about until the end." Tears dripped down Stretch's cheeks as he heard the dying man's wishes.

"I will Lieutenant. You have my word, and I'll tell them to be proud of you too."

"Thanks Captain. Does anyone there know the words to the 23rd Psalm? I want them to pray with me now." He began to slowly recite the words. His voice was soft, but he struggled to get every one out. In his dying moments, as his last good deed on earth, he wanted to lead his brothers in prayer. "The Lord is my shepherd, I shall not want. He makes me lie down in green pastures." Everyone listening took off their helmets, and bowed their heads. Those who knew the words joined in. "Even though I walk through the valley of death, I will fear no evil for you are with me. Surely, goodness and love will follow me all the days of my life, and I will dwell in the house of the Lord forever." Those were the very last words anyone heard from Lieutenant Barnes.

....

As hours turned into days, the number of missing firefighters grew to 343. President Bush declared the events of September 11th, the first war of the 21st century. Through all the turmoil, a love for our fellow man was beginning to grow all over this great country of ours. This event was no more evident, than in the city of New York. If you lived anywhere in the five boroughs of the city, fire-trucks, sirens, and red flashing lights were a way of life. You weren't the least bit affected by it, it blended into the background of life. Most people who lived near the firehouses didn't even notice the building or the men that worked there. This all changed overnight. The city firehouses became shrines for the missing, and a place of comfort for the living. Many people felt the need to mourn even if they did not know a single soul who perished that day. It was their city, their buildings, and their firefighters and police officers who were lost.

Most of the men felt awkward with the new status thrust upon them. People were proclaiming them heroes. They didn't feel like heroes. They were only doing their job. A job they all loved until a few weeks earlier. The real heroes were their brothers who never came home. They made the sacrifice, not them. Around 9:00pm one night, the Margulos visited the Palace. Even though they were dealing with a pain of their own, they came to comfort their friends. The sidewalk was filled with flowers and candles. Lying in the middle of them all were pictures of Richie, Lt. Farley, and Louie Ludwig. They were dressed in their Class A uniforms. The picture had been taken only a few weeks earlier at the funeral for the Probationary firefighter that passed away. How fitting, that the three men who shared so much together in life, were now together in death. It was an eerie feeling seeing the purple and black bunting hanging over the big red bay doors of the Palace. Everyone knew it symbolized a lost firefighter, only this time, it hit closer to home. Three of the very men who worked in this house and protected this neighborhood were now gone.

Before entering the Palace, the Margulos stopped to read some of the cards and notes. There was a teddy bear with a note attached to it. They bent down to get a closer look and to read the note. The note read, "Dear Firemen, Can you please bring this teddy bear to my mom. She was in the building when those bad men crashed into it. She hasn't come home yet, and I know she is afraid. Whenever I'm afraid, she tells me to hug my teddy bear. Please give this to her and tell her I said she could borrow it until she comes home. I miss you mommy. Love, Katie. Oh yeah, daddy loves you too."

The Margulos were not alone. Thousands of people were in the same situation they were. Waiting. Waiting for news. Waiting for news you sensed was inevitable, but didn't want to hear. They had gone to the armory and other places throughout the city and posted pictures of their daughter Annemarie. Maybe she still was alive but hurt somewhere. Maybe, just maybe, someone had seen her. Thousands of pictures were posted throughout the subway stations, parks, and bus stops. Life went on, but it would never be the same. It is hard to forget when you never got to say goodbye.

"Hi grandma, hi grandpa." Joey had greeted his grandparents at the door. He missed his mom and friends tremendously.

"Hi Joey. We've brought some food from the restaurant for everyone. The restaurant had been closed since the attack. Although they still had not reopened, Anthony and Lucille went in today in order to cook this meal for the men. They couldn't just sit back and wait any longer, but they couldn't get themselves to open the restaurant either. There were too many reminders of Annemarie there. They were thankful that Ralphie was there for Joey, but they knew Ralphie hurt also. Their lives had all been torn apart, but they vowed to be there for one another.

....

On September 16, 2001 the FDNY promoted 168 men. Captain Stretch Dolan finally realized his dream of becoming a Battalion Chief. A few men from the Palace went to the ceremony to support their former officer and friend. He was always there for them, and they wanted to return the favor. Stretch was proud to become a Chief, but as he told his wife and family, "No one wants to get promoted this way." Every time he would look at the shiny new gold badge, or his white helmet, he would think of the 343 men that were listed as dead or missing. He would move on from Ladder 179 to a command post in Manhattan, but his heart would always be in Brooklyn. A dentist appointment kept him alive on September 11th. He was glad to be alive, but found it hard to answer the question, why didn't he die also? It simply wasn't his time.

Vinny Amarosa and Bobby Giordano were officially out on medical leave. Vinny had suffered a mild heart attack on the 11th. How ironic, that a heart attack saved his life, and the life of his friend. Bobby Giordano was hit by falling debris, and had suffered a severe concussion. He walked out of the hospital the same day, and right back to the scene. As long as his brothers were buried in the pile, he would be there to help find them. It didn't matter to him what the doctor said. He was the one that had to live with himself, and the guilt of being alive.

Engine 200's rig was completely crushed in the collapse. It took weeks to locate it in all the debris. Although it was parked directly ahead of Ladder 179, it was found 100 feet away. It was a good thing they left Ralphie Junior behind at the Palace that day. In all, 40 department vehicles were lost and had to be replaced. Cities all across the county vowed to replace the rigs. Once again, brothers helping brothers, people giving and not taking.

Ralphie Chiarello not only lost his fiancé that day, but he lost his innocence. His life would be different now. He was a lonely man. Of all the men at the Palace, his world would be affected the most. There would be no more carpools with Richie and Louie, and no more wedding plans with Annemarie.

After the promotion ceremony, the men returned to the Palace. The mood was very somber, as Captain Shields spoke to the men on duty. "We lost some good men the other day. I know it's hard to go forward, but we have to do it for them, and for their families. They would have wanted it that way. Whatever the widows want, consider it done. We need to help them anyway we can. I don't want anyone erasing any names from the assignment board either. As far as I'm concerned, they are still on duty until someone tells me otherwise." At this point he choked up when he looked over to Ralphie. "I'm sorry kid, any news about Annemarie yet?" Ralphie just shook his head and couldn't speak. He wished for a miracle, but it never came. "You sure you want to be here Ralphie. Why don't you take some time off?"

"Lieutenant, I'm sure. There is no other place I would rather be right now. Don't worry about me. I'm o.k."

As the weeks went by, the New York Daily News started to run notices each day of the numerous firefighter, and police officer funerals or memorial services that were taking place during the week. There were so many going on at the same time that the Department asked the public to attend. It was beginning to take its toll on the departments. Joey Donovan and the Emerald Society Pipers were busier that ever before. There were too many services and not enough pipers to go around. Instead of a full band, many of the services had a lone piper play. No man would be forgotten. Each would get a proper send off.

CHAPTER 14

October 4th, 2001

The pile of rubble had by now taken on a new name. It would forever be remembered as Ground Zero. It resembled a nuclear holocaust, and hell on earth. On this day, an event happened to trigger a new beginning. A healing process was about to begin.

Jimmy Valdez had been down at the site almost every day since September 11th. The ironworkers were all working around the clock, cutting through the pieces of jagged steel. They worked with grapplers and welding tools to remove the thousands of tons of steel, one piece at a time. Jimmy's police officer brother was injured on September 11th. His family did not know his condition or whereabouts for 36 hours. He had suffered a broken leg that required surgery.

Richard Damante

When the family heard their brother was alive, they all ran to the hospital to see him. In the meantime, the call went out that ironworkers were needed at Ground Zero. Jimmy proudly answered the call. His job that only a few days earlier seemed unrewarding, had suddenly taken on a new meaning.

For days, everyone at the sight worked diligently to find survivors.

When none were located, their jobs and feelings began to change. There were people, just like them, somewhere in the pile. No one deserved to die like they did. They would find them, and give closure to their families. No one wanted Ground Zero to become the final resting place of thousands. It was a gruesome job, but someone had to do it. Jimmy vowed to be a part of it.

Jimmy had just finished working a 12-hour shift when it happened. Most of the debris had taken on uneven shapes that represented death and destruction. Nothing symmetrical was found in the pile. As Jimmy walked off the pile, he heard a commotion a few feet away. This usually meant another body had been found, and work would come to a standstill. The victim would be placed in a stokes basket, and then draped with an American flag. This time, the noise was not about a body. A large piece of steel in the perfect symmetry of a cross was hoisted from the debris. Immediately, the firefighters and workers dropped to their knees in prayer. The cross was removed intact, and in a ceremony, lifted onto a base. It stood as an inspiration to everyone at the sight. Many had lost their faith that terrible day. They blamed God for not protecting their friends and family members. The cross became a constant reminder that God never left us that day. He was there, and still is today. He is there to comfort the grieving, give strength to the weak, and feed those who are hungry for His word. There are miracles every day on this earth. We are usually too busy to see them. This was God's little way of saying seek me, and you will find me.

....

Emily Risland had been in the intensive care unit since the attack. She had suffered third degree burns on 50 percent of her body. The road to recovery would be a long and slow one. There would be numerous skin grafts, and hours of physical therapy that lay ahead of her. What kept her going through this ordeal was the birth of her daughter Carla. Carla was born two months premature. Her birth date would always be a reminder to her, and the nation, of that terrible day in September.

Emily had been taken to the hospital only minutes after the attack. She was in critical condition, and was even given last rites by a hospital priest. The doctors had no other choice but to deliver her baby by caesarian section. It was the only way both the mother and child would have any chance of surviving. For two weeks Emily lay in a coma. She knew nothing about the fate of her husband or baby. She remembered hearing voices, and then seeing bright, peaceful, comforting lights. A few times, she was tempted to let herself go. She wanted to see what was on the other side of the lights, but each time, she came back. When she finally awoke from the coma, she asked for her husband and baby. She remembered nothing about the attack, or what had happened to her. When she was stable, the doctors broke the news about Carl, and then brought in Carla for her to see. She wept both tears of sadness and joy. She knew how much Carl wanted to be a dad, and now, he would never get the chance. His daughter was beautiful. She had Carl's eye and hair color. There was no hesitation when it came to naming her daughter. Baby Carla was named after her daddy. The daddy who would never get the chance to hold her, and tell her how much he loved her. Carla was one of 10,000 children who lost a parent that day.

Emily begged the nurses to let her hold Carla. Her fingers and hands were badly burned, and heavily wrapped in bandages. Her motivation to get well lay in a five pound baby girl. For some reason, God decided to take Carl from her, but he also gave her a daughter. She would forever be grateful for this gift of love.

....

As days turned into weeks, Ralphie began to cope with the death of his fiancé. He searched for comfort in the Margulos, and in Joey. Ralphie and Joey would never get to have the father and son relationship they both desired. Joey moved in with his grandparents, but spent every chance he got at the Palace. In an effort to ease the pain from losing his mom, the men gave Ralphie Junior to Joey. They loved the dog, but Joey needed him more than they did right now. Before going to school, Joey would drop the dog off at the firehouse each day, and then take him home at night. Ralphie Junior had the best of both worlds. He had a boy to love him and play with, and all the excitement Dalmatians craved, down at the Palace.

Deep within, Ralphie felt like a failure. In Annemarie's time of need, he wasn't there to help her. The injury to his shoulder may have saved his life, but it stole his self- respect. Like the other survivors, the question he asked himself everyday was why not me? Why did God choose me to live? He felt both guilt and anger at the same time. After weeks of praying, the answer finally came to him one afternoon. He was at the Palace and feeling depressed. He had not missed a single day of work since September 11th. He left himself no time to grieve for Annemarie and his brother firefighters.

The Palace doorbell rang. Ralphie got up to answer it and found Joey waiting for him. It was then that he realized his prayers were answered. It all made sense now. Joey became just like a little brother to Ralphie. His life was spared in order to help Joey. He had lost his father years ago, and now his mom. Ralphie would be there for Joey. They both sat down and talked. They talked about Annemarie and they shared a good cry. Through her death, they would become best friends, and closer than ever before. One life, once again touching another.

CHAPTER 15

October 22, 2001

As the city tried to heal from the events of September 11th, a wave of patriotism took the country by storm. American flag sales grew so large, that the manufacturers could not keep up with the demand. Anywhere you traveled, from the farmlands of Kansas, to the lakes of Minnesota, or the desserts of Arizona, American flags flew proudly. The nation felt New York's loss. We are all Americans, and too many had died at the hands of the terrorists. We would fight a war like no other in all of history. There were no uniforms to identify the enemy. They were here in America, across Europe, and spread throughout the Middle East.

The New York Yankees were once again playing for the American League pennant. They provided relief from the daily grind that had overtaken the city. There had not been any survivors found at the site since the first few hours after the collapse. The search and rescue mission had now been changed to a recovery mission. The families found it hard to give up hope. They wanted closure, but felt it hard to deal with the reality. One by one, the heavy steel beams were being removed. It was tedious, and it seemed like it would never end.

A group of 307 new firefighter recruits reported to duty today to begin their training. These men faced challenges like no other time in Department history. They were hired to fill the vacancies caused by the events of September 11th. Vacancies were easy to fill, but the recruits could never fill the shoes of the men who were lost. Hundreds of years of experience were wiped out. Some of the lost were from what the Department called the war years, the years of the 1970's and early 1980's when the FDNY responded to more alarms than any other time in history. They were chiefs, officers, firefighters, and men from all five Rescue Companies who were now gone. The Department could never replace that experience.

Among the 307 new recruits was Andrew Jenkins, the son of Alan Jenkins. Andrew had taken the Fire Department test a few years earlier. He had a good job working as an Advertising Executive in a midtown-advertising agency. Andy had started to climb the corporate ladder, and now made more money than at any other time in his life. At 29, he was one of the oldest recruits in his class. What he lacked in firefighting experience, he would make up for with desire.

The Jenkins family took Alan's death very hard. They were all looking forward to the family vacation with their dad, when he was suddenly taken away from them. It just didn't seem fair. Andrew had no desire to become a city employee. He had taken both the police and fire tests just to make his dad happy, but now, it was different. Andrew knew his dad died trying to help others live. He decided to follow in his dad's footsteps, and wanted to give, just like Alan had always done. In honor of his father's memory, Andrew vowed to become the best firefighter he could be. The cut in pay didn't matter. It wasn't about the money. It was all about his dad, his principles, and his own way to heal.

Back at the Palace, things just weren't the same. Richie, Lieutenant Farley, and Louie Ludwig were all missed. Vinny Amarosa was home recovering from his heart attack, and Stretch Dolan had been relocated to another area of the city. Every tour, the Department signal 5-5-5-5, for box 8087, was sounded. The four 5's was to inform the men of a firefighter death. The men would listen intently to hear the names. They each knew some of them by name, but many more by sight. The only way to heal would be to move forward. Life goes on no matter what the circumstances may be. We are only a small part of the universe that surrounds us all.

....

Jane and the kids decided it was time to visit the Palace and clean out Richie's locker. Through daily prayer, the family was finally able to accept Richie's death. He died doing what he loved. They knew by their faith, that many rewards awaited Richie in heaven. They talked about what his final minutes of life would have been like. Jane, Amanda, and Tommy found comfort in knowing Richie wasn't alone when the end came. They had heard that Richie, Lt. Farley, and Louie had all been spotted together minutes before.

It was a typical autumn day in New York. The leaves had turned golden brown, and began to blanket the ground. Nature was getting ready for another season. The trees and flowers would become dormant in preparation for another northeast winter. Since Ralphie had the day off, he decided to pick up Jane and the kids, and drive them to the Palace. It wasn't a long ride, but what the heck, anything he could do to help, he would.

"Hi Ralphie, thanks for doing this. I don't know if we would have been up to driving back by ourselves later. You've been a good friend to all of us. How are you doing these days?"

"I'm, I'm…. I'm hanging in there," Ralphie stuttered. He had been dealt a terrible hand in recent months. His life was turned upside down all in the span of one morning. The men at the Palace began to worry about him. He still refused to take any extra time off of work. Captain Shields told him he needed to let his emotions out. Instead, he kept them bottled up inside. It was the only way he knew how to cope right now.

"Hey Ralphie, can I drive," Tommy shouted.

"Go sit in the back Tommy. Ralphie's got it taken care of."

"Come on mom, I know he'll let me drive his car."

"Listen to your mom Tommy, it's okay. I'll let you drive next time."

Tommy and Amanda piled into the back seat. As the car wound through the traffic on the Belt Parkway, the conversation turned to memories of Richie and Annemarie. "Richie was the first guy at the Palace I became friends with. He kinda took me under his wing. He used to kid around with me a lot, but it was all good natured stuff."

"He really enjoyed the rides home from work with you and Louie. What did you guys talk about?"

"Usually, we would talk about our families. He always said nice things about you Jane." She smiled and her eyes began to tear. She cried for Richie everyday. They were tears of love, and of emptiness. She had lost her best friend. "You know, he really loved all of you."

"Dad was so excited the day he came home and told us you and Annemarie were getting engaged. I think he wanted to go with you guys that night and be there when you popped the question."

"You know what Amanda, I never got the chance to ask him to be my best man at the wedding. He was like a big brother to me."

"He would have been honored Ralphie. It would have meant a lot to him." As Jane said these words, a silence came over everyone in the car. Each person was deep in his or her own thoughts.

The silence then turned to sighs, and then to smiles and laughter. Memories were what made people go on living. Without memories, there would be nothing to hold onto.

The ride to Brooklyn was a ride back into time. They passed Coney Island, and the Verrazano Bridge. Off in the distance stood the Statue of Liberty. What a sight she was. She still held vigil over the harbor. Miss Liberty was a symbol of America, and everything America stood for. She beckoned the early immigrants to come to America for a better way of life. In the early 1900's, thousands of people passed her daily on their way to Ellis Island. The city had been built on the blood and sweat of many of these people. The Statue still held her head up high, but she also cried for our nation. From her vantage point in the harbor, she had a clear view of the attack on September 11th. There were even rumors that she had been a target that day.

As they exited the Brooklyn Queens Expressway at Hamilton Avenue, Jane and her children began to feel anxious. They passed the familiar neighborhood sights. There was Saint Stephen's Church, the park, and Giovanni's Restaurant. It had been a long time since all of them had visited the Palace, but the neighborhood hadn't changed a bit. The only noticeable difference was that of American Flags flying proudly from every building in the neighborhood.

Ralphie turned the corner, and there was the Palace. The large bright red bay doors were open, and Engine 200, and Ladder 179 were parked on the apron waiting for action. The men had washed and shined the rigs for their special visitors today. Engine 200 was an old replacement rig on loan from the fire academy. It would be months before the new one would arrive. Ralphie Junior saw the approaching visitors and ran to greet them. He wagged his tail and barked his greeting.

Jane and the kids walked by Ladder 179. Mounted on the wall next to the rig was the rack where the firefighters hung their gear. There were three empty spaces where Lt. Farley's, Louie's, and Richie's gear would have been. The emptiness told the story. They continued on to the steps that would take them upstairs to the day room, kitchen, and sleeping quarters.

"Hi Jane, hi there kids. It's great to see you." Bobby Giordano was on house watch. He chose his words carefully, and really didn't know what to say. "I'm glad you came by today. I see Ralphie Junior already introduced himself to you."

"Oh yeah, we heard so much about this dog. You know what Ralphie, he does look like you."

"You're just like your dad Tommy, always kidding around."

They passed the daily assignment board located right next to the house watch post. All the names from September 11th were still on the board. As they climbed the stairs, they passed by all the company pictures. Richie would always be a part of this firehouse. His life would be remembered not by the way he died, but by the way he lived. He was a man of integrity, and a friend to all that knew him.

The men were all waiting for Jane and the kids. Captain Tom Baker was the first to greet them. He had recently been promoted, and was Stretch Dolan's replacement. "Hi Jane, I'm Tom Baker, nice to meet you. Hi kids." He cleared his throat and continued on. "I knew your dad for a long time. I actually taught him back in the academy. Been to a lot of fires together over the years. He was a great fireman, and an even greater guy. He'll be missed. I wish I would have had the chance to work with him here."

"Thanks Captain. I appreciate the kind words. We're all going to miss him a great deal."

"We sure are going to miss his cooking around here. Jimmy Lennon's spaghetti and meatballs just aren't the same as Richie's," Joey Donovan shouted. The laughter broke the ice, and before you knew it, an hour had passed. They all laughed and cried, and told stories about their missing brothers.

Ralphie put his arm around Tommy's shoulder and took him to Richie's locker. Tommy opened the door and saw the pictures of his mom, sister, and himself on the locker door. A wood cross hung on the back wall. Written below it was a sign. It was Richie's favorite bible verse. "For God so loved the world, that he sent his only begotten Son, and all who believe in Him, shall not perish, but have eternal life." John 3:16.

Tommy read the sign and had to fight back the tears. They were tears of joy. He knew his dad was in a better place, but he also missed him very much. They were very close. He would be the man of the house now at a young age. He knew his dad would count on him to help take care of his mom and sister.

One by one, Tommy started to pack Richie's belongings into his duffle bag. When he got to his official department work shirt, he paused, and decided to wear this one. It was his to keep. He grabbed the old FDNY baseball cap that was his dad's favorite, and placed it on his head. When he was finished, he went to remove the cross and bible verse, but decided to leave it there for the new guy who would someday be assigned this locker. Maybe, just maybe, it would change that person's life.

"Oh my, you look just like your dad." Tommy smiled as he heard Jane's words. Seeing him standing there wearing Richie's hat and work shirt brought back a lot of memories. He looked like a carbon copy of his dad. Jane remembered how proud Richie was the first time he put on his uniform. He promised never to do anything to embarrass his family, or the Department. Needless to say, it was a promise he kept until the very end.

CHAPTER 16

January 1, 2002

Christmas had come and gone. It was a difficult time for everyone. Many of the victims still had not been found or identified. Instead of the annual Christmas party at Giovanni's, the Margulos held a Celebration of Life party. Anthony and Lucille went out of their way for their friends. The walls of the restaurant were decorated with pictures of Annemarie, Lt. Farley, Richie, and Louie. Three months had passed, and their bodies still had not been found.

Jimmy Valdez had reported to work early on New Years morning. For the last four months he had worked long grueling hours. Days had gone by since any victims had been found. The ironworkers would move the large steel beams, and the firefighters and police officers would climb into the voids to search. The work was monotonous, and gruesome at times. Jimmy had just finished cutting through a large piece of steel. The grapplers hooked it, and hoisted it off the pile. In a scene repeated many times over the last few months, the firefighters moved in and began to search.

"Hey, I think we got something, Chief. Come here, quick." Jimmy watched as the man in the black coat and white helmet went in to check. He radioed for the work around him to stop. Yes, they had definitely located a body. Usually, a find like this would turn up other victims. In a matter of minutes, three more bodies were located.

"Chief, it looks like we found some more of our men." Stretch Dolan heard this and climbed down the hole for a closer look. He had been filling in down at Ground Zero for the last few weeks. As he climbed down the narrow opening, he flashed his light and saw the familiar neon yellow reflective stripes that were sewn onto every firefighter's turnout coat, and bunker pants. There was no mistake, some brothers had just been found. As he got closer, he also saw two helmets. On the front of two of the helmets were the red shields signifying these men were part of a ladder company. As he bent down to pick the helmet up, he immediately froze, and began to shake his head from side to side. He tried to compose himself as he read the number on the shield. It was still legible, and it read 179. He knew right away that he had found two of his own men. The third helmet was found a few feet away. It had a white shield with a single ax, and the number 179 in the middle. It was Lt. Farley's helmet. The bodies of Richie, Louie Ludwig, and Lt. Farley had just been found. They were lying in a huddle. They stayed together until the very end.

Stretch Dolan could not contain his emotions any longer. He was a friend of each of these men. He was now a Department Chief, but he still was a man. He cried like never before. After a few minutes, he picked up his radio and called dispatch. He notified them that three men, all from Ladder Company 179, had just been found. Department procedure called for the company to be notified. They would then ride to the scene and carry their fallen brothers out. As the saying was told over and over through the last few months, they never leave a brother behind.

"Firehouse, Fireman Amarosa." Vinny took the call and notified Captain Baker immediately. He notified all the men present from both companies. Although Richie, Lt. Farley, and Louie were all assigned to the Ladder Company, the men from Engine 200 also wanted to be a part of the ceremony. They lived and worked with these men for years. They shared the same quarters, and were not going to let the numbers on their helmet shields dictate what they could and could not do in this situation. Ralphie took the news the hardest. Tears fell down his cheeks, and he began to weep uncontrollably. For the last three and a half months he kept most of his emotions bottled up inside, but it was now time to let go. After gaining his composure, he called Jane and told her the news. They were thankful that Richie could now have a proper burial. The news also brought back the painful reminder of what took place that awful day in September. The wounds that were beginning to heal would be open once again. It was bittersweet, but in the long run, they all knew this day would one day come. Jane hung up the phone and called her kids into the kitchen. "I have some news for you, they just found your dad. His friends from the station are going there now. We need to plan a funeral."

"Mom, can we go down there also?"

"Do you want to Amanda?"

"Yeah, I think we all do. We know dad is in heaven, but I need to be there."

"Me too Mom, lets go."

"O.k. Tommy. I'll call Ralphie and tell him we want to be there also."

Before the men from the Palace and the families of the fallen firefighters arrived, the remains were put in a stokes basket, and each of them were covered with an American flag. Each man would be treated with dignity and respect. Stretch Dolan made sure of that. Finding bodies was something you never got used to, but you did it anyway. Finding your friends was a different story altogether. What kept Stretch going, were the thoughts of the families. They would finally be able to sleep at night, knowing their loved ones had been found. Closure would come soon.

Before hopping onto the rigs for the short ride across the Brooklyn Bridge, the men gathered for a moment of silent prayer. Their tears would be shed now, and not in front of the onlookers and families at Ground Zero. "Come on boys, let's go bring them home," Captain Shields shouted. The rigs rolled down the apron into the narrow streets of Brooklyn Heights. Ladder 179 led the way this time. As the rigs turned onto Cadman Plaza, and the entrance to the Brooklyn Bridge, each man was deep in his own thoughts. They were about to ride back in time to a day none of them would ever forget. This time, their mission was different. There was no fire to put out, or civilians to rescue. This was a personal mission.

Each man braced himself for what was about to happen. They didn't know how they would react, or if they could even live up to the task at hand.

When the families arrived, the men from Ladder 179 and Engine 200 walked down into the pile. A department Chaplain was on hand, and Joey Donovan brought his bagpipes. An order was given, and all work stopped. Every firefighter and ironworker present took their helmets off, and bowed their heads. "These three men are our brothers. We knew them as co-workers, as friends, and as firefighters. Their families knew them as the fathers, husbands, brothers, and sons that they were. Today, my reading is from the gospel of John. Jesus told the apostles, my command to you is this. Love one another as I have loved you. Greater love has no man, that he lay down his life for his friends." He nodded over to Joey, and Joey began to play. He had played this song so many times before, but this time would be different. He looked skyward and uttered the words, "Richie, my friend, this one's for you brother." As the notes came out, they sounded different than any other time he had played this song. Amazing Grace took on a whole new meaning to the men at Ground Zero today. They sang the words, and for the first time, many felt the true meaning. Richie's faith in God was a major part of his life, and now it would be a part of his brothers' lives. Every life has a meaning, each one touching another.

As the flag draped baskets were carried from the pile, every man and woman present saluted. They slowly walked to the waiting ambulances. This scene would be repeated over and over in the next few months, as more firefighters were found. Ralphie's last thought this evening was for Annemarie. He knew she was in there somewhere. To be this close, and to not find her, made him angry. Tonight would be another sleepless night. It would be months before he would have a good night sleep again.

On May 30, 2002, a ceremony was held as the last steel column was removed from Ground Zero. There were no more bodies found. Annemarie, Carl Risland, Alan Jenkins, and Bill Vogler's families would never have the chance to say good-bye.

On June 1, 2002 the FDNY Medal of Valor was posthumously presented to the 343 men who lost their lives on September 11, 2001. Every department member who was at the World Trade Center between the hours of 8:46am and 10:28 am received the Survivor/Rescuer Ribbon.

Richard Damante

On June 3, 2002, in response to the communication problems with the radios, the FDNY announced plans to test a new $14 million system.

CHAPTER 17

September 11, 2002

An emotional ceremony was held at Ground Zero to mark the one- year anniversary of the attack. Life and death came full circle this day. Emily Risland returned to the scene for the first time. She brought her mom, and her daughter Carla with her. Carla Risland would celebrate her first birthday while thousands commemorated this tragic day.

Emily's emotions ran high today. On one hand, she was happy to be alive, and happy that her daughter was doing well. On the other hand, she missed Carl tremendously. She still needed around the clock help doing life's routine things, but it made her stronger. Her strength came from her desire to someday hold Carla in her arms, and to be a good mom to her. Her physical scars would never go away. She prayed that one day her emotional ones would.

The families who attended were led to the bottom of Ground Zero. Ralphie, Joey, and the Margulos walked down with the others. The President was there, and had a private time with the families. Some families brought flowers and mementos, and laid them on the ground. Ground Zero had become a large, dusty, concrete hole. All of a sudden, a gentle wind began to swirl and it picked up the dust and papers from the bottom of the hole. Just like the steel cross, the wind was a sign of God's presence once again. God never left us after all. As the calm wind swept across the pit, it touched everyone in its path. The hand of God was there to provide comfort to His children. There were many tears shed on both September 11, 2001, and September 11, 2002. Some of them were tears from heaven. We were created in God's image, and told to love one another. Somehow, not everyone heard the message.

EPILOGUE

Somewhere in the world, history is repeating itself once again. A little boy watches in excitement as a bright red fire truck passes down the street. The red lights are flashing, and the siren is wailing. The deep blasts of the air horn sound out as the truck approaches the busy intersection. The boy now sees the men who are riding inside the cab. They are all dressed in their firefighting gear. They are wearing their black coats and boots, and heavy leather helmets.

Every time the boy hears the familiar roar of the diesel engine, he will imagine himself someday riding the truck to a call. He will dream this dream many times, and someday, it will become a reality. You see, no one chooses the fire service as a career. It chooses you. Somewhere up in heaven there is a special place where these decisions are made. It is a place where the firefighters of days gone by go for rest. Their lives had been cut short by the sacrifices they made. Lieutenant Farley, Richie, and Louie Ludwig are all there. They must be planning something big, because so many were called home on September 11, 2001.

No one knows the reasons why this tragic event happened. It is not for us to ask why. It is up to us to prevent it from happening again. God knows the feeling of sadness. He knows what it is like to lose a child. Our God is a God of hope, and of love. The next time life becomes too heavy to keep on going, remember God will be there for you. God created all of us for a specific purpose. Use your gifts wisely. Dream big, and place your faith in God.

THE TOLL

What effect did the attack on the World Trade Center have? Here are some startling facts.

- 1 out of every 33 people on the FDNY force died on September 11th, (343 of 11,400)
- American Flight 11, 92 lives lost
- United Flight 175, 65 lives lost
- 80 nationalities represented among the dead and missing
- 10,000 children lost a parent on September 11th, 2001
- WTC death toll, 2,617 as of January 25, 2002

WORLD TRADE CENTER FACTS AND FIGURES

The World Trade Center was the brainchild of developer David Rockefeller. The towers restored lower Manhattan at a time the area was in decline. The area he chose to build the towers was called radio row. It was made up mostly of electronic stores and small retail shops. 164 buildings were demolished to make room for the 16-acre site. Over 10,000 people worked to build the towers. There were 60 deaths during construction.

- North Tower opened in December 1970
- South Tower opened in January 1972
- The World Trade Center complex consisted of 7 buildings
- Home to two subway stations and the New Jersey Path trains
- Had the largest air-conditioning plant in the world

- 1WTC supported a 110 meter television and radio antenna
- Over 43,000 windows in the both towers
- The North Tower stood 417 meters tall
- The South Tower stood 415 meters tall
- The buildings ranked as the fifth and sixth tallest buildings in the world at the time of their destruction
- 50,000 people worked in the buildings
- An estimated 200,000 people visited them daily
- The complex had its own zip code
- Each tower had 97 passenger elevators
- In 1993 terrorists tried to bring the buildings down with a truck bomb that they parked in the basement. Over 1,000 people were injured, and 6 people were killed

"The World Trade Center is a living symbol of man's dedication to world peace."

Architect Minoru Yamasaki,
the buildings designer

THE BROTHERHOOD

I became a firefighter in February of 1980. In God's big picture, the reason I became a firefighter was different than mine. I thought that becoming a firefighter meant helping others. I was right, but the helping would be more powerful than I ever imagined. Now, twenty years later, I finally know why.

I grew up in a typical, middle class, Long Island family. Long Island is made up of many different small towns. Each town has its own Fire Department. I joined the Garden City Fire Department when I was 19 years old. I was assigned to the Ladder Company. Not knowing much about department operations, I was a little disappointed with my assignment. I wanted to be the nozzle man on the hose line, but that was the job of the Engine Company.

As time went by, I was glad to be a "truckie". A truckie is what firefighters call members of the Ladder Company. The Engine and Rescue Companies get all the glory, but the Ladder Company does all the hard work. (Yes, I'm biased.) I know no one ever put out a fire with a ladder, but trust me; we make the lives of the Engine guys a lot easier by getting in front of, and on top of the fire. In a fire, all the hot air and poisonous smoke rises. It is the Ladder Company's job to gain access to the building, conduct a search and rescue, and vent the fire.

I never forget the first real fire I went to. I had been to a few car fires, and oven fires, but never to a fully involved building. My first "signal 10", (Nassau County radio code for a confirmed working fire), was at the Stewart Manor Train Station. It was in the early hours of a Sunday morning. The temperature was just above the freezing point, making things more difficult. I knew I was part of the team when my Captain told me to grab and ax, and head to the roof with him. People always ask me if I was afraid, but I honestly wasn't. The adrenaline was flowing, and I was with a bunch of guys who knew what they were doing.

As the roof saw started to roar and cut away at the roof, thick black smoke started to ooze from the cuts the saw was making. With the pick head of the ax, I pulled back the roofing shingles and the plywood beneath them. I immediately got a face-full of what was inside. With all the precision of a highly trained unit, the roof was opened the very moment the Engine Company got water on the fire burning below us. If the roof were opened too early, it would provide the needed oxygen the fire needs to grow, and pull the fire upward into the ceiling and roof.

I finally felt what it was like to be a firefighter. Before this night, the biggest thrill I had was riding on the back step of Ladder 147 to false alarms.

After the fire was out, it was our job to perform the overhaul duties, and check for any small pockets of fire that may still be burning. During overhaul, everyone kind of lets their guard down and relaxes a bit. Maybe that is why most firefighter injuries occur during overhaul operations than in actually fighting the fire.

Before we climbed down the roof ladder, the Captain gave me a pat on the shoulder and told me I did a good job. I was finally accepted into the "Brotherhood" of firefighters. I looked out over the roof to the east, and saw one of the most beautiful sunrises I had ever seen. Most people in the neighborhood slept through the early morning excitement. Such is the job of a firefighter. People take them for granted. They know they are there, but never really think about them unless they need them.

I would continue to be a firefighter for 10 years. During those 10 years I never once thought about quitting. Getting out of a warm bed in the middle of the night was no big deal. It was fun. I was also very proud to wear the uniform. It made me feel special. Eventually, I got married and moved to another town. I transferred and became a member of the West Hempstead Fire Department. Over the years, I responded to many calls. I may not remember the names of the victims, but I still remember the faces, especially those of the children. Firefighters all have big hearts. When they have children of their own, their hearts become even bigger.

I eventually achieved the rank of Lieutenant, and was assigned to Engine 761. Engine 761 was an old Mack pumper. It was the second due engine at all fires in town, and the first due on all mutual aid calls outside of our district. I missed being in the Ladder Company, but I loved my new assignment. At about the same time I became Lieutenant, we put a brand new 100-foot tower ladder in service. A tower ladder is like a portable elevator. It has a ladder you can climb, or you can hop in the bucket attached to the end of the ladder, and ride it straight up. We were having a drill one Sunday morning, and all of us were taking turns riding in the bucket. The higher up we went, the view became larger. When the ladder was fully extended we were over 100 feet in the air. What a view.

As I looked to the east, north, and south, I saw the vast expanse of Long Island suburbia. There were many homes, but no tall buildings except for Nassau County Medical Center to the East, and the North Shore Tower Apartments to the North. Over 20 miles away in the west, the Manhattan skyline silhouetted against the rising sun. In the center of the skyline stood the Empire State Building. Moving to the right was the smaller but distinguishable Chrysler, and Citicorp buildings. All the way to the left, standing proud in all their glory, were the sparkling Twin Towers of the World Trade Center. What an awesome sight.

Growing up in New York, many of us took for granted what people came from all over the world to see. We could see the skyline everyday if we wanted to. Like most New Yorkers, I had visited the towers, but never took the time to go to the top of the building. It would be a decision I would regret later on in my life.

Manhattan is a unique place. It is only one and a half miles wide, and twelve miles long. It is home to people from every country, and every religion known to man. It truly is a melting pot. New York

City is made up of five unique boroughs. The northern most borough is the Bronx, followed by Manhattan. Brooklyn and Queens are located just east of Manhattan. Staten Island sits across the bay from Brooklyn and to the south. The men and women of the FDNY and NYPD protect the millions of people who live and work in the five boroughs. Many fire and police practices across the country have come about due to the actions of the FDNY and NYPD.

I am proud to be a member of the brotherhood of firefighters. I know that I can walk into any firehouse across this great country of ours and be treated like a member of the family. I also know that many firefighters have a feeling of invincibility about them. Many also have a spiritual side to them, and do answer to a higher authority. They believe in God, but their faith is tested by the very nature of their job.

September 11, 2001 tested my faith, and the faith of many others. In a matter of minutes, the FDNY lost 343 of their bravest. Among the lost that day were Chiefs, a Chaplain, Captains, Lieutenants, Firefighters, and men from each of the five Rescue Companies that responded to the call. For days, all I could think about were these heroes, and their families. I thought about what they might have been thinking climbing up those stairs, when thousands were heading in the opposite direction.

God put this story in my heart. My 10 years of firefighting experience was there in order for me to write this book. He gave me the words. I wrote No Greater Love for two reasons. I ask you to remember these reasons as you go on in your daily lives. First, never forget the actions and sacrifices my brother firefighters made on September 11th. Second, and more importantly, remember this one thing above all others. It will help you in good times and in bad times. It will help you cope with any situation you encounter. It is the basis for our lives, and our very existence.

"For God so loved the world that He sent His One and only Son, and all who believe in Him Shall not perish, but have eternal life."

John 3:16

THE FIREFIGHTER'S PRAYER

When I am called to duty
Wherever flames may rage,
Give me the strength to save a life
Whatever be its age.

Help me embrace a little child
Before it is too late,
Or save an older person from
The horror of that fate.

Enable me to be alert
And hear the weakest shout,
And quickly and efficiently
To put the fire out.

I want to fill my calling and
To give the best in me,
To guard my every neighbor and
Protect his property.

And if according to God's will
I have to lose my life,
Please bless with your protecting hand,
My children and my wife.

ABOUT THE AUTHOR

Rich Damante was born and raised in New York, and became a firefighter when he was 19 years old. He served in two departments, and attained the rank of First Lieutenant. His passion for firefighting, and for his faith, provided the inspiration needed to write this story.

Rich has also written four full length dramas. Three of them have been performed in Scottsdale, AZ. All of his works are stories of hope. He has lived in Scottsdale since 1989. It is the love of his wife Joann, and their 18 year old twins that keep inspiring him to pursue his writing.